Complexity in Second Language Study Emotions

This book offers a socially situated view of the emergence of emotionality for additional language (L2) learners in classroom interaction in Japan.

Grounded in a complexity perspective, the author argues that emotions need to be studied as they are dynamically experienced and understood in all of their multidimensional colors by individuals (in interaction). Via practitioner research, Sampson applies a small-lens focus, interweaving experiential and discursive data, offering possibilities for exploring, interpreting and representing the lived experience of L2 study emotions in a more holistic yet detailed, social yet individual fashion. Amidst the currently expanding interest in L2 study emotions, the book presents a strong case for the benefits of locating interpretations of the emergence of L2 study emotions back into situated, dynamic, social context.

Sampson's work will be of interest to students and researchers in second language acquisition and L2 learning psychology.

Richard J. Sampson (PhD, Griffith University) has been working in the Japanese education context for more than 20 years. He is currently an Associate Professor at Rikkyo University, teaching courses in English communication and language learning psychology. His research focuses on the social and dynamic emergence of language learner and teacher psychology by drawing on complexity thinking. He uses action research approaches to explore experiences of classroom language learning from the perspectives of students and teachers. Richard has published widely in international journals and is the author of "Complexity in Classroom Foreign Language Learning Motivation: A Practitioner Perspective from Japan" (Multilingual Matters, 2016), and co-editor (with Richard Pinner) of "Complexity Perspectives on Researching Language Learner and Teacher Psychology" (Multilingual Matters, 2021).

Routledge Research in Language Education

The *Routledge Research in Language Education* series provides a platform for established and emerging scholars to present their latest research and discuss key issues in language education. This series welcomes books on all areas of language teaching and learning, including but not limited to language education policy and politics, multilingualism, literacy, L1, L2 or foreign language acquisition, curriculum, classroom practice, pedagogy, teaching materials, and language teacher education and development. Books in the series are not limited to the discussion of the teaching and learning of English only.

Books in the series include:

Complexity in Second Language Study Emotions
Emergent Sensemaking in Social Context
Richard J. Sampson

Performed Culture in Action to Teach Chinese as a Foreign Language
Integrating PCA into Curriculum, Pedagogy, and Assessment
Edited by Jianfen Wang and Junqing (Jessie) Jia

Virtual Exchange for Intercultural Language Learning and Teaching
Fostering Communication for the Digital Age
Martine Derivry and Anthippi Potolia

Technology in Second Language Writing
Advances in Composing, Translation, Writing Pedagogy and Data-Driven Learning
Edited by Jingjing Qin and Paul Stapleton

For more information about the series, please visit www.routledge.com/Routledge-Research-in-Language-Education/book-series/RRLE

Complexity in Second Language Study Emotions
Emergent Sensemaking in Social Context

Richard J. Sampson

LONDON AND NEW YORK

First published 2023
by Routledge
4 Park Square, Milton Park, Abingdon, Oxon OX14 4RN

and by Routledge
605 Third Avenue, New York, NY 10158

Routledge is an imprint of the Taylor & Francis Group, an Informa business

© 2023 Richard J. Sampson

The right of Richard J. Sampson to be identified as author of this work has been asserted in accordance with sections 77 and 78 of the Copyright, Designs and Patents Act 1988.

All rights reserved. No part of this book may be reprinted or reproduced or utilised in any form or by any electronic, mechanical, or other means, now known or hereafter invented, including photocopying and recording, or in any information storage or retrieval system, without permission in writing from the publishers.

Trademark notice: Product or corporate names may be trademarks or registered trademarks and are used only for identification and explanation without intent to infringe.

British Library Cataloguing-in-Publication Data
A catalogue record for this book is available from the British Library

Library of Congress Cataloguing-in-Publication Data
A catalog record has been requested for this book

ISBN: 9781032308449 (hbk)
ISBN: 9781032308456 (pbk)
ISBN: 9781003306955 (ebk)

DOI: 10.4324/9781003306955

Typeset in Times New Roman
by Deanta Global Publishing Services, Chennai, India

Contents

List of figures		vii
List of tables		viii
Acknowledgments		ix
1	The emotionality of additional language learning	1
2	From simplicity to complexity: Recent explorations of L2 study emotions	13
3	Interactions between the whole and parts in the emergence of L2 study feelings	26
4	Focusing a small lens on experiential and discursive context	43
5	Co-adaptive emergence of emotional intersubjectivity	54
6	Widening the lens: The (re)construction of anxiety and enjoyment	63
7	Widening the lens: L2 study emotions and agentic personality	72

| 8 | Weaving threads for researching | 86 |
| 9 | Pedagogy for emotionally charged educational spaces | 95 |

Appendix   105
References   106
Index   119

Figures

3.1 Compilation of number of references to feelings by lesson segment over the semester (the scale is by tens of references)   37

3.2 A multiple threading representation of a readers' theatre performance (adapted from Davis and Sumara [2006]). The horizontal axis is time, while the vertical axis is threads of discussion. Each horizontal row represents a thread of the discussion, with overlaps and recurrences   39

3.3 Feelings multiple threading for learners over the semester. Rows represent individual learners, while columns pertain to lessons. The different shading represents instances of different feelings mentioned in reflective journals for each lesson for that learner   40

Tables

2.1	Contributions of recent L2 study emotion research	24
3.1	Feelings, working definitions, and examples of coding to each	32
3.2	Degree of occurrence of feelings across learner journals, percentage of students mentioning feelings, and feelings co-occurring	34
3.3	Lesson segments involved in the focal course	36
4.1	Transcript of part of Keiko and Tsutomu's short conversation	51
5.1	Transcript of part of Keiko and Tsutomu's short conversation	58
6.1	Transcript of Akito's main speaking turn during short conversation	67
7.1	Transcript of part of Kazuma, Makito and Wakana's short conversation	75
7.2	Transcript illustrating Makito and Wakana's relationship	80

Acknowledgments

The empirical work that forms the basis of this book concerns a particular group of additional language learners. Naturally, I am indebted to these young adults for their willingness to join me in exploring the emotional experience of classroom study. I also, however, recognize that, in the absence of interactions with numerous prior groups of students, I would not have developed such an interest in the psychological and social dimensions of language learning. My gratitude, therefore, extends to all the learners with whom I have had the privilege of working over my teaching career. I hope to build on the understandings you have helped me to fashion.

Like any academic work, my ideas have also emerged via various discussions and interactions with colleagues. Richard Pinner has been integral in pushing my work forward, whether it be through explicit dialogue on practitioner research and the psychology of additional language learning, or merely (?) shooting the breeze. In fact, we recently realized that, despite living within reasonable distance of each other, our interactions have almost entirely consisted of online chats and only the occasional coffee in the material world. Here's hoping we can get together for that long-planned family barbecue at a point not too far in the future. I am also indebted to Ema Ushioda, whose kindness, occasional emails and chats, and conceptual, methodological, and ethical contributions to the area of additional language learning and teaching have been an inspiration. Ema was also the insightful soul who put me in contact with Richard P. in the first place! While they have grown less frequent over the years as I shifted my place of work, I am deeply appreciative of many a Robson's chat with Sylvain Bergeron. I remember excited flurries of exchanges as our discussions headed into uncharted territory, our ideas truly feeding off each other. I am, moreover, much obliged to a range of people with whom I have interacted less often, but whose support, comments, or ideas came when I needed them most: James Carpenter, Sal Consoli, Olivier Elzingre, Joe Falout, Atsushi Iida, Saeko Machi, Ryo Nitta, and Reiko Yoshida. I offer my thanks to the members of the QIRC collective – sharing perspectives on data and the process of researching classrooms has been invaluable, and I hope that we can continue to learn from each other. I include my deep gratitude to Katie Peace at Routledge, for offering me the chance to discuss this project at a conference in Australia, under that brilliantly deep blue sky, and for assisting me along the way to seeing this in print.

I would like to extend my appreciation to certain organizations: First, to the Japan Society for the Promotion of Science (JSPS) for the kakenhi grant-in-aid (19K13258) that assisted with conducting this research. Second, to the academic journal *Studies in Second Language Learning and Teaching* for being able to re-use text from earlier versions of sections of this book appearing as Open Access (Attribution 4.0 International) in Sampson, R. J. (2022). "Shifting Focus through a Small Lens: Discursive and Introspective Perspectives on the Emergence of L2 Study Emotions" 12(1), pp. 15–36.

Last but not least, I send my love to my family here in Japan. Although the opportunities for monster gokko have decreased over the years, it is a wonder to see my children grow (further) into the wonderful human beings they are. No doubt supported by the wonderful model that their mother lives.

1 The emotionality of additional language learning

"How are you?"

Despite the fact that the standard response to such a greeting might often be the rather opaque and superficial "I'm fine", the ubiquity of the inquiry says something important about emotions. They form such a fundamental part of our everyday lives that, upon meeting another, emotions are one of the very first topics we raise. We care about emotions – our own and those of the others around us. They are ever-present in human life (Cahour, 2013; Immordino-Yang, 2016), essential to our complex experience of everything from the quotidian to the exceptional.

As one increasingly commonplace aspect of the lives of many around the world, the field of additional language (L2) learning seems to be witnessing a growing emotional charge. While perennial in the research landscape, empirical work investigating L2 study emotions has proliferated since the turn of the century and specifically in the past decade (Dewaele, 2019). Such an upturn is also represented in academic journals through special issues (e.g., Studies in Second Language Learning and Teaching, 2018) and sections (e.g., Modern Language Journal, 2019) devoted exclusively to emotions in second language acquisition (SLA). For L2 educators, it looks like there may be good reason for such an increase in empirical work: Contemporary affective neuroscience is uncovering that "most of the thought processes that educators care about, including memory, learning, and creativity, among others, critically involve both cognitive and emotional aspects" (Immordino-Yang & Fischer, 2016, pp. 86–87). Based on an extensive neuroscientific research program, Immordino-Yang (2016) urges that "for school-based learning to have a hope of motivating students, or of producing deep understanding, or of transferring into real-world skills … we need to find ways to leverage the emotional aspects of learning in education" (p. 18).

Developing an additional language is an emotional journey, as anyone who has worked with learners or gone through the process themselves will,

DOI: 10.4324/9781003306955-1

no doubt, attest. Yet, in spite of an extended history of research in this area, intriguing questions remain: In what ways do learners' emotions emerge in interaction with different aspects of classroom activities? How do the dynamic range of emotions experienced by individuals come together to form the emotional climate of a class group over time? How could exploring the different perspectives and contributions of individuals in communicative interaction enlighten our understandings of the social emergence of L2 emotions? What colors of the life history and personality of an individual might interact with their (social) actions and emotional experiences in present L2 learning and usage contexts? In considering such dimensions, this book aims to illustrate one way of furnishing more holistic yet detailed, social yet individual understandings of the emotions of people learning in L2 classrooms.[1]

Emotions are ...

Without venturing to label it a "definition", Izard (2010) draws on a survey of 34 highly respected researchers to offer the following "pluralistic description" of emotion:

> Emotion consists of neural circuits (that are at least partially dedicated), response systems, and a feeling state/process that motivates and organizes cognition and action. Emotion also provides information to the person experiencing it, and may include antecedent cognitive appraisals and ongoing cognition including an interpretation of its feeling state, expressions or social-communicative signals, and may motivate approach or avoidant behavior, exercise control/regulation of responses, and be social or relational in nature.
> (p. 367)

In terms of dealing with emotions in this book then, at their most fundamental, emotions are viewed as responses to interactions with the world around us. They are episodes which occur via a stimulus known as an object or event focus (Shuman & Scherer, 2014). Past research has revealed the important role in educational contexts of emotional object foci connected to activities and outcomes, information processing during tasks, contents or topics of learning, social relationships with classmates and teachers, and events outside the direct learning environment (Pekrun & Linnenbrink-Garcia, 2014). Although the stimuli that may most commonly come to mind are those from the present (such as anxiety during a presentation), emotions can also be situated in our memories of events (such as embarrassment upon remembering a past social failure) or our imaginings or future prospections (for example, through anticipation of meeting a cherished friend) (Baumgartner et al., 2008). In fact, based on affective neuroscience, proponents of the theory of constructed emotion contest that we place too much emphasis on thinking of "triggers" in the external environment:

> Emotions are not reactions to the world. You are not a passive receiver of sensory input but an active constructor of your emotions. From sensory input and past experience, your brain constructs meaning and prescribes action ... and sometimes that meaning is an emotion.
> (Feldman Barrett, 2018, p. 31)

Emotions also comprise different components, perhaps the most often considered of which are our subjective feelings, "the *perception* of a certain state of the body along with the *perception* of a certain mode of thinking and of thoughts with certain themes" (Damasio, 2003, p. 86 – emphasis added). They additionally involve physiological reactions (such as blushing in embarrassment and changes in heart rate), expressive behaviors which facilitate the conveyance of emotional information to others in social settings (most commonly witnessed in facial expressions and body posture), and tendencies toward action (Cahour, 2013; Damasio, 2003; Flack & Laird, 1998; Shuman & Scherer, 2014). In this sense, emotions are integrally intertwined with motivations through "creating dispositions, orienting not only action but also thinking and the way of being in the world" (Cahour, 2013, p. 67).

Emotions have, moreover, been classified in various other ways in the literature. For instance, it has been claimed that the emotions of anger, disgust, fear, joy, sadness, and surprise have universal forms of expression (Ekman et al., 1972). Popular culture has embraced such ideas, as in the 2015 animated film *Inside Out*. Diverse qualities of emotions can also be considered, such as their valence, intensity, degree of consciousness, and duration (Cahour, 2013). Concerning valence, emotions have typically been classified as positive or negative depending on whether they are experienced as pleasant or unpleasant (Pekrun, 2014), with the former fostering broad tendencies to build resources and the latter triggering "fight or flight" action (e.g., Fredrickson, 1998; Plutchik, 2001; Shuman & Scherer, 2014). That said, valid arguments have also been made that blind assignment of emotional valence is unhelpful, in that such oversimplification "ignores outcomes for particular people in a range of real contexts" in which "'positive' or 'negative' emotions might create unexpected results" (Oxford & Gkonou, 2021, p. 53).

Importantly for L2 learning, emotions and social interaction form a complex, integrated system whereby one cannot be separated from the other.

In this sense, "which emotion surfaces is neither determined solely by the context nor by an individual's psychological tendencies, but by the organismic interplay of the two" (Boiger & Mesquita, 2015, p. 383). Accordingly, emotions are functional to particular social and cultural contexts. Emotional experience and behavior will emerge in phenomenologically divergent ways in different circumstances with different interpersonal relationships (Mesquita & Boiger, 2014). As Järvenoja and Järvelä (2013) conclude from an extensive program of studying classroom group-work, the regulation of emotions "is embedded in the collaborative learning context, in group members' reactions to each other and in the nuances of these reactions", and "cannot be assigned to any individual alone" (pp. 176–177). In terms of the emotionality of L2 learning, there is, thus, an implication to look at "the dialectic between the individual and the social; between the human agency of these learners and the social practices of their communities" (Norton & Toohey, 2001). Such a dialectic is also evident in the confluence of emotional experiences connected with L2 study through which my own interest has emerged.

Arriving at emotions, arriving at this book

As Miyahara (2015) wonders: "It is somewhat surprising that not many researchers make transparent their journeys as learners, teachers or researchers. Rarely do we find information about them in their writings, yet we are expected to read, contemplate and discuss their research" (p. 177). Research outcomes might be better understood in the context of the processes through which they evolved, processes which include relevant facets of the life history of a researcher – in this case, my emotions connected with L2 study.

My first encounter with L2 learning occurred as a 13-year-old in an Australian secondary school. Forced to select from an extremely limited range of elective subjects for a semester, I opted to study French. With regret and profound apologies to the teacher concerned, my younger self really could not make a connection with a language that appeared to have almost nothing to do with my life in semi-rural Australia. The lessons seemed to drag on interminably, and I found myself on the verge of dropping off to sleep on numerous occasions. At other times, I recall taking glee in making sure I articulated with an embarrassing crudeness the vast array of new vocabulary items that our teacher modeled beautifully (yet endlessly). Needless to say, while I had the option to continue French, my excursion into additional language study took an extended break after this first dalliance.

A number of years later, as an undergraduate, I shared an apartment with my twin brother. Commencing his university studies later than I, he had returned to Australia from a year spent studying abroad in Mexico. Fluent in Spanish, yet with almost no outlet for this new-found identity, my brother decided to press his learning on me. Each morning before he set off for the university at which he studied, he scribbled seemingly cryptic messages with an accompanying vocabulary key. Morning after morning, I would carry these notes to my own university, curiously deciphering them on the bus ride. As my language developed, my brother and I would take great joy in watching Spanish-language films, listening to Mexican music, and being able to sit in public places and talk with each other in a language we felt sure nobody around us could understand. Such was my progress with Spanish that, when I undertook the traditional Australian pilgrimage to Europe after graduation, I was able to savor a feeling of achievement in communicating with people in Spain and even Italy – albeit admittedly falteringly!

Shortly afterward, as a young adult, I shifted to Japan for what I intended to be a brief period of work. Regardless of what should have been an awakening to the intrinsic enjoyment and instrumental utility of L2 learning through my experiences with Spanish, naively I studied not a word of the Japanese language before I set out. Rather surprisingly, I managed to get by for a time – I was surrounded by expats who had lived in the country for longer than I and upon whom I could rely to interact in Japanese instead of me. As I had no plan to stay in Japan for a prolonged period, I could see little value in learning the language. As time passed, however, my expat friends came and went, I changed my place of work to a junior-high school in which Japanese was requisite, and ... fell in love! My plans were naturally revised, and I started to study the language little by little. As I made the effort to live and learn Japanese in-country, I suffered the embarrassment of failing to get my meaning across in any number of contexts; tasted the joy of understanding utterances in the local dialect; felt anticipation as I wrote diary entries with increasingly complex linguistic features, knowing that I would show them to my Japanese girlfriend when next we met. I felt a strong sense of unease when not studying or using Japanese. Reading books in my native English was a waste of time; I read only in Japanese. Starting from children's picture books and simple novels, I experienced the exhilaration of becoming able to read literary works, such as the books of Haruki Murakami and Banana Yoshimoto, within the space of a couple of years. I was obsessed. Japanese *was* my identity. (Interestingly yet sadly, my fond relationship with the language has turned 180-degrees after the birth of my Australian-Japanese children and their overwhelming use of Japanese rather than English, the association of Japanese with mundane clerical tasks of my working life, and a gradual realization of the attrition of my native language).

Over my time in Japan, I have also worked constantly as an L2 teacher in diverse educational contexts – private *eikaiwa* (English conversation) schools, elementary and junior-high schools, a college of technology, public adult education, and my current position in the university setting. No doubt based in my own L2 history, something that has long intrigued me is how the people with whom I interact in the classroom feel about different learning experiences and emotionally connect with their L2 studies. Day in and day out, I have worked alongside learners whose emotions bubble to the surface in any number of different ways, expressed through a multitude of forms, seemingly triggered by disparate events. Some students in a group laugh and raise their voices as they enthusiastically plan the plot for a short video presentation, while learners in another group with the same task sit in strained silence, rolling their eyes. The conversation of a pair of students stops and starts as they try desperately to express themselves about a topic one week, as the same pair rapidly exchange utterances, growing progressively more excited about a topic the following week. As I share a selection of photographs upon return from an overseas conference, some students look intrigued, oohing and aahing at various scenes; others switch from looking at the photographs to their desks in polite boredom; while still other learners, who did not express observable interest during the lesson, send an email afterward to share with me their feelings of relatedness in having visited the same places.

As I have become increasingly fascinated by the variety of emotionality in my classrooms, I have also progressively taken steps to foster empirical insights into the experiences of L2 learners. Building on past studies (Sampson, 2019b, 2020, 2021; Sampson & Yoshida, 2020, 2021), this book, thus, presents research with students in my English as a foreign language (EFL) lessons at a Japanese university. This practitioner research works to move away from an overly simplistic view of L2 study emotions.

Complexity in life, complexity in (L2) psychology

Morin (2008) discusses simplicity as involving disjunction, in separating that which is linked, and reduction, in unifying that which is diverse. The history of research into L2 study emotions has, in cases, provided a study in disjunction, through a rending of emotions from other psychological processes, exacerbated by further atomization to a single factor: It is dominated by language anxiety (Horwitz et al., 1986). Indeed, Pavlenko (2013) contests that such has been the fascination with this lone dimension, it has led to a dearth of scrutiny of other aspects of the emotional landscape. Moreover, while L2 learning is a dynamic process conducted by specific individuals, both disjunction and reduction are conspicuous in past studies which have tended to utilize survey methods to advance static snapshots averaging across populations. As MacIntyre and Vincze (2017) admit, the quantitative nature of much research means "it is not known to what extent emotions experienced by individuals … mirror the group-level patterns reported" (p. 82). Finally, disjunction is again evident in a neglect of recognizing the complex psychological beings in learning spaces as interacting with other complex psychological beings, that is, the separation of emotions from emergent social context (Pavlenko, 2013). It follows that there is a necessity to "give up the handy and neat notion of modular ID [individual difference] factors" arising from a simplistic worldview, and rather "reframe learner characteristics in a more fluid and dynamic manner" (Dörnyei, 2017, p. 80). What I thus aim to show in this book are some possibilities for exploring, interpreting and representing the lived experience of L2 study emotions in a more holistic, complex fashion.

Diane Larsen-Freeman (1997) first introduced complexity thinking to applied linguistics with a seminal article focusing on language itself as a complex system, as well as emphasizing the nonlinear, unpredictable, and chaotic nature of L2 development. The following decades have witnessed the continued application of complexity ideas to SLA and applied linguistics in general (Ellis & Larsen-Freeman, 2009; Hiver & Al-Hoorie, 2020; Larsen-Freeman & Cameron, 2008; Ortega & Han, 2017a). More specifically, side by side with numerous journal articles, complexity perspectives have been used to push forward considerations of L2 learner and teacher psychology through edited volumes (Dörnyei et al., 2015; King, 2016; Sampson & Pinner, 2021) and research monographs (Pinner, 2019; Sampson, 2016).

Complexity thinking forms a foil to the simplistic worldview. As exemplified, to a degree, by some of the previous research focusing on L2 study emotions, much of our thinking has been socialized into a kind of mechanistic simplicity, the idea that we can understand something by separating and reducing and that we can generalize and predict based on understandings of the parts (Doll, 2012; Morin, 2008; Osberg et al., 2008). In contrast, complexity perspectives encourage us to regard phenomena as:

> A fabric (complexus: that which is woven together) of heterogeneous constituents that are inseparably associated: complexity poses the paradox of the one and the many … Complexity is in fact the fabric of events, actions, interactions, retroactions, determinations, and chance that constitute our phenomenal world.
>
> (Morin, 2008, p. 5)

Complexity thinking prompts us to understand that it is nonsensical to look at the constituent parts of many phenomena in isolation, out of time and context – we need to look at the parts and the whole in interaction over time in specific contexts. It is through the interactions of elements – the "threads" – that novel, emergent phenomena arise – the "pattern" of the fabric. As Simpson and Rose (2021) astutely analogize,

> if a biologist were aiming to understand how a certain type of plant grew simply by observing the plant, but failed to consider either the growing medium, or nutrients, they would be neglecting a significant element of what fosters plant growth.
>
> (p. 138)

Complexity can involve its own unwieldy amount of perhaps mystifying terminology (although I would also argue that the *concepts* themselves are most likely not all that unfamiliar to most classroom practitioners and researchers – see also Pinner & Sampson, 2020). Unfortunately, there can be a tendency to obfuscate what ought to be illuminating possibilities with an overload of such technical terms or, indeed, a mistaken belief that people need, thus, to be described as "systems". While, clearly, much is lost in taking an extract out of its context, the following quote serves as an apt example: "It must be noted that while … the L2 developmental system is closed rather than open, individual learners should strive to keep their systems as open as possible" (Han et al., 2017, p. 227). I could well imagine the young people in my classrooms cocking their heads to one side in open bewilderment if I urged them to "keep their systems as open as possible"! As Ushioda (2021) has also cautioned, "such discussions of human behavior can create … something of a 'distancing' effect, where individual intentionality, reflexivity and decision-making become transmuted into mathematical models representing abstract systems above the level of the individual person" (p. 274).

My take on complexity aligns with Larsen-Freeman's (2017) understanding of it as a metatheory; it offers epistemological, ontological, and axiological guidance. Or, as Ortega and Han (2017b) put it, a "conceptual framework that provides broad theoretical and methodological principles for how to judge what is meaningful (or not), acceptable (or not), and central (or not) in the task of building knowledge about a phenomenon" (pp. 2–3). To this end, rather than overwhelming with a cascade of specific terminology (some shall be necessary, though I hope to introduce it in a relatively straightforward manner), the way that complexity is utilized in this book is as a reminder of more integrated, holistic understandings of the psychology of additional language learners.

Complexity research requires a focus on real people in ecologically valid settings (Ushioda, 2015) and takes a strong focus on dynamics and the ways in which phenomena evolve over time (Gleick, 1987). Take a moment to contemplate a few aspects of an L2 learner's experience of everyday life: At every step of the way, they live their lives intermeshed in many interacting layers. Psychologically, an individual is never purely a motivated person or an emotional person, much less simply an anxious person. Although they might have certain tendencies to action and thinking, they will express these colors of personality or identities differently in different situations with different associated emotions. An "L2 learner" is only one of a variety of identities they will perform, and any additional language aspects may connect more or less with other dimensions of their everyday lives (Ushioda, 2009). They are also living through time, as their own unique past (psychological) experiences and future prospections interplay with their current (psychological) interactions. Moreover, their psychology is in continual interaction with the dynamic social situations in which they are located and help to co-form. Complexity urges us to remain cognizant that "the continuous interactions among the myriad of inter-personal and intra-personal processes are intricate, nuanced, contextualized and ever-changing" (MacIntyre et al., 2021, p. 16).

Regarding emotions in particular, as Cahour (2013) comments, "we are constantly in the process of feeling something, in a more or less intense way. And being-in-the-world in a certain affective rapport whose fluctuations are frequent and subtle" (p. 58). We will naturally *feel* something through expressions of (or constraints on) our personalities, identities, motivations, and so on. Our emotions will also play a part in co-forming the (social) context for interactions, just as they will feed back into understandings of experiences in a social context as well as our evolving psychology (Sampson, 2019b). Almost four decades ago, Denzin (1984) argued that the research of emotionality

> requires a situating of the phenomenon of emotion back in the world. By contextualizing, the investigator places and studies emotion in the world of lived experience. Emotion is located in the personal biographies of interacting individuals. Contextualizing isolates its meaning for them, presenting it in terms of their languages, meanings, and understandings.
>
> (p. 10)

While Schumann (2015) astutely emphasizes that in complexity approaches to exploring human psychology "the individual is the entity of concern, and case studies become recognized as the appropriate level of granularity" (p. xvi), regarding the focus of the current book, he is only partially correct. Emotions need to be studied as they are dynamically experienced and understood in all of their multidimensional colors by individuals *in interaction*. In this book, I draw on complexity thinking to locate interpretations of the emergence of L2 study emotions back into a situated, dynamic, social context.

What the book offers

As with all research monographs, it is perhaps unlikely that a reader might progress from cover to cover, following the sequential order of pages. That said, in line with my ideal of including my own voice as practitioner researcher, I intend to make my writing as narrative as possible. Therefore, there will be theories, ideas, and metaphors that I introduce more fully earlier on in the narrative of my journey through exploring L2 study emotions, those that I return to again and again, and others that develop detail as my understandings expand. Nevertheless, I here include a brief outline of each chapter for those who might be more inclined to dip and choose to read only selected portions of the book.

Building on the foundations laid out in the first chapter, **Chapter 2** provides a selective review of more recent empirical work focusing on L2 study emotions. Broadly, the featured research covers the expansion to look at emotions other than anxiety, such as enjoyment and boredom; the sheer diversity of emotions experienced in L2 study; the fine-lens view offered by idiodynamic methodology; the connections between L2 study emotions and other aspects of psychology, such as motivation and personality; and situated case studies revealing identity and social aspects to L2 study emotions. Concordant with the stance of the book, I draw on a number of challenges to and hopes for the investigation of L2 study emotions recognized over the years (Arnold & Brown, 1999; Dewaele, 2021; Pavlenko, 2013) to consider the ways in which the reviewed research offers more contextualized, dynamic insights.

Chapter 3 commences the empirical section of the book. I begin by offering detail about the context, participants, and implementation of the classroom research which also forms the basis for the following four chapters. I then detail my initial analysis which focused somewhat of a wide-angle lens on the whole and parts, so to speak. The chapter presents general findings about the kinds and degree of feelings noted by learners in the context of their L2 studies with me and the connection of these feelings to certain segments of each lesson. It is in the context of this exploration of emotionality during particular parts of lessons that my decision to center on the discursive emergence of emotions in social interaction occurs. I finally describe the use of a tool known as *multiple threading* (Davis & Sumara,

2006) to gain an appreciation of the range of emotionality experienced by both individual learners and the class group across a semester as a whole.

Following the aim of the book to more adequately contextualize L2 study emotions, along with Ushioda's (2009, 2011a, b) long-standing pleas for more empirical work which considers social context, **Chapter 4** introduces and then exemplifies a *small-lens approach* (Ushioda, 2015, 2016). The chapter works to display the benefits of looking in more detail at the emergence of emotionally significant experiences or critical incidents (Tripp, 1993) for a selection of learners as case studies. While focusing on a particular instance of emotionality, the analysis combines discursive data illuminating the social context with the experiential perspectives from introspective data of group members. The case presented reveals the non-linear emergence of emotional sense-making. Although not the primary focus, the case also serves to uncover some of the teleological (or functional) dimensions of emotions in social situations.

Chapter 5 continues my illustration of the use of the small-lens technique. The analysis revolves around a seemingly incongruous emotionally significant episode for two learners: Feelings of enjoyment and relatedness during a short conversation from a starting point of discussing experiences of disappointment. In particular, the chapter highlights the co-adaptive emergence of emotions and emotional intersubjectivity (Denzin, 1984) as the students co-create the discursive and emotional context via their social interactions. The analysis reveals the ways in which the interlocutors move away from an overt discussion of disappointment by drawing in various shared transportable identities (Zimmerman, 1998) in conjunction with expressing dimensions of common Japanese (L1) conversational style while interacting in their L2.

Both complexity perspectives and Ushioda's (2016) small-lens approach remind us of the prominence of historical context in understanding a phenomenon of concern. In **Chapter 6**, then, I widen the lens to include such aspects, as I present my analysis of a significant emotional event, this time, for an individual learner. The focal case revolves around understanding more about his seemingly synchronous experience of anxiety and enjoyment. Exploration of his reflection leads me to include not only consideration of the present discursive and experiential context but also the historical setting for this event and the ways in which it reverberated to foster salients (Kauffman, 2008) for his narration of present emotional experience of action.

The final empirical addition to the book, **Chapter 7** further widens the temporality of the research focus. I once more home in on an individual learner, starting with a reflection in which he remarked upon an experience of intense personal achievement via his time in the classroom on a particular day, and especially with regard to the short conversation session. While I continue to explore the discursive context for this experience, I moreover uncover examples of the non-linear impact on current emotionality of the focal-student's relationships with group members and myself as teacher as well as his lifelong understandings of personality. The chapter draws attention to the people in classrooms as not only "L2 learners" but as agentic individuals who make (emotional) sense based on their own histories and personalities.

Chapter 8 commences my conclusion of the book by bringing together my thoughts connected with researching based on the various accumulated cases. The chapter summarizes the implications for future empirical work of taking the kind of holistic approach to L2 study emotions adopted throughout the book. I also reflect upon the benefits, limitations, and challenges of taking a small-lens approach to investigating L2 study emotions. In the hope of encouraging others to more seriously consider the function of social context in the emergence of emotions, the chapter, moreover, includes a range of suggestions for further research in this area.

Given my dual role as a researcher and practitioner, **Chapter 9** rounds off the book by offering a selection of pedagogical insights. Of note, I argue that the findings presented herein serve as a reminder for teachers to remain cognizant of the rich emotional landscape to any class group; to consider the possibly varied ways in which emotions connect to different segments of lessons and, in particular, those in which compulsory (commercial) textbooks are used; to realize that both pleasant and unpleasant emotions can have constructive (or unconstructive) functions; and to allow opportunities for learners to notice and share their emotions and transportable identities (Zimmerman, 1998) to the degree that they deem appropriate.

Note

1 While I believe I have been quite clear already, I should state that this book concerns "L2 *study* emotions". That is, I am considering emotions emergent in the course of formal study of an L2 in a classroom setting. This is, however, certainly not to say that I am focused purely on some kind of special "L2 emotion" (such as language anxiety). In line with the holistic perspective, I am interested in any and all emotions that arise as my learners interact in the classroom (which happens to be an L2 classroom, with learners happening to be interacting in an additional language). This focus is also in contrast to examining, for example, the emotionality of L2 learners or users in online or naturalistic contexts, as well as the ways in which emotional expression differs across languages.

2 From simplicity to complexity
Recent explorations of L2 study emotions

Traditionally, the field of SLA emotions has been subsumed under the all-encompassing bracket of "affective factors", including such additional psychological aspects as motivation, self-confidence, and willingness to communicate. Writing just before the clock chimed at the end of the previous and the start of the new century (and around the same time that I was beginning my extended "short visit" to Japan), Arnold and Brown (1999) remarked on the importance of gaining broader understandings in this area:

> Attention to affective aspects can lead to more effective language learning. When dealing with the affective side of language learners, attention needs to be given both to how we can overcome problems created by negative emotions and to how we can create and use more positive, facilitative emotions. … As we teach the language, we can also educate learners to live more satisfying lives and to be responsible members of society. To do this, we need to be concerned with both their cognitive and affective natures and needs. … Attention to affect can improve language teaching and learning, but the language classroom can, in turn, contribute in a very significant way to educating learners affectively.
>
> (pp. 2–3)

Despite such hopes, in the following years, Pavlenko (2013) was quite critical of the way that the "affective factors paradigm" had "exhausted its limited explanatory potential" (p. 6). In terms of emotions, she argued that traditional approaches overly focused on the single factor of language anxiety, obsessed with a search for the holy grail of linear cause-effect relationships between emotion (in many cases conflated with anxiety) and language achievement and were disturbingly neglectful of social context (Pavlenko, 2013, pp. 7–8). Regrettably, published more than 20 years after Arnold and Brown's (1999) initial call, Dewaele (2021) equally feels that L2 emotion research has been retarded because of ongoing questions of how to do justice to its study. He calls attention to challenges regarding methods to "capture" emotions in unequivocal ways, how to disentangle emotions from other aspects of L2 development, useful timescales upon which to focus, and what dynamic qualities of emotions might most usefully be investigated (p. 208).

Perhaps in recognition of such hopes and challenges emergent throughout its history, recent L2 study emotion research has marked a noteworthy diversification: Dewaele, MacIntyre, and colleagues (e.g., Boudreau et al., 2018; Dewaele & Alfawzan, 2018; Dewaele & MacIntyre, 2014, 2016) have expanded their focus to examine relationships between language anxiety and L2 learning enjoyment; Simsek and Dörnyei (2017) present an intriguing look at anxiety through the lens of an ecological model of personality; and other specific emotions such as boredom (Pawlak et al., 2020a) are gaining attention. A handful of studies offer more situated, qualitative interpretations in classroom (Garrett & Young, 2009; Gkonou, 2017; Imai, 2010; Méndez López & Peña Aguilar, 2013; Sampson, 2019b) and online social contexts (Sampson & Yoshida, 2021; Yoshida, 2020; see also chapters in volume edited by Freiermuth & Zarrinabadi, 2020). Additionally, there are moves to furnish a dynamic view of L2 study emotions via idiodynamic case studies (Boudreau et al., 2018; Gregersen et al., 2014, 2017) as well as research illuminating the "veritable rainbow of feelings perceived by learners" (Sampson, 2020, p. 207).

The current chapter, therefore, spotlights certain of these contemporary studies which take a broader and more complex approach to investigating the emergence of L2 study emotions. It must be stressed that this is not intended to be a comprehensive literature review but, rather, affords a general idea of the directions in which empirical work in this area is moving away from the simplism of the affective-factors paradigm. Moreover, I ought to point out that my placement of studies under distinct headings is more for ease of reading than strict categorization – there is clearly overlap in the areas focused upon in many of these research reports. Regardless, throughout the review, I urge the reader to consider the ways in which these new research directions address or shine light upon the previously noted hopes and concerns raised by Arnold and Brown (1999), Pavlenko (2013), and Dewaele (2021).

Anxiety and the move to studying other emotions

By far the most richly researched of L2 study emotions, language anxiety is considered a unique and situation-specific worry or nervousness connected with learning and using an L2 (Horwitz et al., 1986). In a valuable overview of its approximately 40 years of exploration, MacIntyre (2017) summarizes a range of reported academic, cognitive, and social causes of language anxiety; such diverse triggers as unrealistic learner beliefs, methods of testing, biased perceptions of proficiency, personality traits, cultural gaffes, and competitiveness in classroom activities are merely a few (p. 21). The inability to present ideas to the same level as in one's native language, and perceptions of negative evaluation by others such as teachers and peers have been commonly linked with anxiety through threatening self-image (e.g., Dewaele & Alfawzan, 2018; MacIntyre & Gregersen, 2012). Dewaele and Alfawzan (2018) also found that negative practices and comments by teachers frequently connected with anxiety and decreased self-confidence in participants' L2. Other effects of language anxiety include increased thoughts of failure and self-deprecation, impediments to language input, processing, and output, and thus decreased willingness to communicate in social learning settings (MacIntyre, 2017). As MacIntyre and Gregersen (2012) conclude, "one of the most consistent findings in the SLA literature is that higher levels of language anxiety are associated with lower levels of language achievement" (p. 103). It can, moreover, push individuals to the point of giving up on learning an L2 completely (Dewaele & Thirtle, 2009).

Empirical efforts focused on language anxiety have undoubtedly established its injurious nature while offering a multitude of pedagogically crucial insights over the years. However, as I have previously, perhaps overcynically remarked, "such is the extent of this literature that one could be forgiven for believing anxiety to be the default feeling for any L2 learner" (Sampson, 2020, p. 204). It would appear that we, as researchers, also have begun to realize there might be more going on in classrooms than a desolation of steadily anxious learners: Moves toward positive psychology perspectives on L2 learning (MacIntyre et al., 2016) have coincided with an enlarged focus on language anxiety and *enjoyment* (e.g., Boudreau et al., 2018; Dewaele & Alfawzan, 2018; Dewaele & MacIntyre, 2014, 2016). For instance, Dewaele and MacIntyre (2016) detail a large-scale study in which 1,742 multilinguals from around the world, spanning 11 to 75 years of age, responded via internet survey. The survey of mostly closed-ended items asked participants to mark on a five-point Likert scale about their anxiety and enjoyment in L2 classes. In addition, there was also an open-ended question encouraging respondents to detail their feelings during an especially enjoyable episode from L2 classes. Counterintuitively perhaps, analysis of the quantitative data intimated that L2 anxiety and enjoyment function separately from one another. As Dewaele and MacIntyre (2016) summarize on the basis of their analysis, these emotions "do not necessarily operate in a seesaw relationship, where one goes up and the other goes down, but rather they function somewhat independently" (p. 230). A combination of the quantitative and qualitative components of their study also uncovered some of the detail of L2 enjoyment in social and private dimensions – positive feelings from encouraging and supportive peers and teachers and an internal sense of pride through succeeding in the face of challenges.

On the other side of the emotional coin, recent years have also seen a blossoming of research into a concern no doubt fundamental to learners and teachers worldwide: that of the potential for boredom. Pawlak and associates (Pawlak et al., 2020a,b, 2021) are championing these exploits with learners in Poland. Pawlak et al. (2020a) specifically explored the object foci of boredom for more than 100 advanced (English major) undergraduates studying at universities in Poland. Through analysis of a Likert-scale questionnaire, these researchers unearthed different foci to participants' boredom that they termed "reactive" – stemming from monotony and repetitiveness – and "proactive" – made up of a lack of challenge and stimulation in classes. Pawlak et al. (2021) then took an intriguingly focused and dynamic look at the "boredom trajectories" of three such undergraduates over the space of three lessons. Data were collected via numerous timescales through a one-time boredom questionnaire, a boredom grid filled out at 5-minute intervals during lessons, and written reflections completed after each session. Although there were naturally more detailed variations by individual, all three participants showed a tendency to increasing boredom over the space of each lesson. The researchers also found that the students were more or less bored dependent on the topic of each lesson – topics through which they could feel a connection between the classroom and everyday life were less likely to elicit boredom – and their expectations for learning – activities that were undemanding, predictable, and required little attention quickly elicited boredom (Pawlak et al., 2021, p. 12).

Variety of emotions

The need for expansion to consider L2 study emotions other than purely anxiety is additionally represented in my own research, revealing what I intrinsically understood as a teacher already – classrooms (and other learning contexts) are a dynamic melting pot of ever-shifting emotions. In one study (Sampson, 2020), I actually set out to gain a better understanding of the social construction of *motivation* for EFL learners in my university classes through action research. Yet, while I did uncover insights into this area (Sampson, 2017, 2018, 2019a), I was surprised to find that the data I collected seemed to, in fact, shout the *emotionality* of my students' experiences. Hence, I revised my analysis of the journal data of 47 Japanese undergraduates to focus on instances of feelings and connected object foci over one semester of L2 study. Even grouping references together, I found they remarked upon seven pleasant (a sense of achievement, enjoyment, gratitude, interest, admiration, excitement, surprise) and three unpleasant feelings (disappointment, a sense of difficulty, anxiety) across a breathtaking 94% of the total collected responses. In support of the turn to positive psychology (MacIntyre et al., 2016), pleasant also eclipsed unpleasant feelings in this classroom setting. Crucially, one of the main insights, though, was the diversity and dynamicity of feelings that learners within the same classroom reported experiencing. Even though there were some common object foci, such as learning activities, peers, and L2 and transportable identities (Zimmerman, 1998), students' feelings diverged connected with similar object foci in the same lesson; there was additionally ambivalence of feelings by the same individuals within the same activity, lesson, and over the semester (Sampson, 2020, pp. 207–211).

Shortly after this study, I was fortunate to be able to organize and conduct research with a researcher in Australia, Reiko Yoshida, into the feelings experienced by participants through an online L2 text-chat exchange (Sampson & Yoshida, 2021; see also Sampson & Yoshida, 2020 for a more focused treatment). Twenty-one undergraduates studying EFL with me at a university in Japan, and 19 Japanese as a foreign language (JFL) undergraduates studying with Reiko at a university in Australia participated. In the chat sessions, learners messaged each other for 30 minutes in one language, then 30 minutes in the other, such that they had opportunities to use both their L1 and L2. Longitudinal, qualitative data was collected over seven chat sessions through reflective session reports. The findings, presented in Sampson and Yoshida (2021), again revealed a multitude of feelings experienced through the L2 online chat. For pleasant feelings, enjoyment was most prevalent for the JFL group and interest for the EFL group; conversely, for unpleasant feelings, both groups remarked upon mixes of frustration and a sense of difficulty most frequently. Despite being in a very different social context to the classroom, the results also supported those from Sampson (2020). In both the EFL and JFL groups, mentions of pleasant feelings amounted to more than double those of unpleasant emotions. Moreover, there was, at times, great diversity across the students as to how different emotions connected with different object foci, yet in other senses, similar patterns of dynamics across the exchange (as in anxiety giving way to interest giving way to boredom over the seven sessions).

Idiodynamic research

The increasing recognition of the fluctuating dynamics of L2 study emotions in some of this empirical work (e.g., Pawlak et al., 2021; Sampson, 2020; Sampson & Yoshida, 2021) is also the specific purview of research which takes a so-called "idiodynamic" approach (MacIntyre, 2012). This research method involves a participant being video recorded while conducting an activity of interest, then immediately watching the recording and rating, for example, their self-perceived anxiety second-by-second using special computer software, and finally using stimulated recall (Gass & Mackey, 2000) to inquire as to reasons for the self-ratings. As one may expect, the approach has been employed most vigorously by its originator, Peter MacIntyre, and his associates for explorations focusing on willingness to communicate (MacIntyre & Legatto, 2011), language anxiety (Gregersen et al., 2014), and interactions between language anxiety and enjoyment (Boudreau et al., 2018).

One such idiodynamic study in which MacIntyre was involved (Gregersen et al., 2017) provides useful hints toward interpreting expressions of emotions. Inspired by a need to support teachers in their ability to discern (and assist) anxious language learners, these researchers embarked upon an investigation of the differences in reading of non-verbal language anxiety cues. The study drew on video recordings and idiodynamic analysis previously conducted in Gregersen et al. (2014) with three highly anxious and three least-anxious Spanish as a foreign language (SFL) undergraduates from the United States. In that phase of the research, following the idiodynamic method, these learners had been video recorded giving an oral presentation in their Spanish class, directly after which they had watched the video of themselves and self-rated moment-to-moment fluctuations in the level of their language anxiety. The second phase of data collection, which is the focus of Gregersen et al. (2017), revolved around asking a language teaching professional and a fellow SFL student to watch the same videos and also rate the anxiety levels for these learners. The researchers then compared these self (presenter), expert, and peer-ratings, as well as what auditory and visual non-verbal cues converged or were dissimilar in interpretations of language anxiety across the three perspectives. Suggesting that anxious learners may overthink the potential for others in the classroom to pick up on their nervousness, the first case analysis showed that there was far greater variation in intensity of anxiety perceived by the students themselves than either their peers or the teacher. Regarding non-verbal cues, across the three types of observers there were 14 presenter behaviors noted consistently (such as furrowed brows and rocking forward representing increasing anxiety), but none of the presenters exhibited all of these behaviors. In addition, there was far more congruence between cues noticed by the students themselves and the teacher (47 behaviors!) than with the peer observer (16), implying that the teacher's previous classroom experience may have been vital in identifying hints of language anxiety. Nevertheless, Gregersen et al. (2017) encourage language practitioners to become familiar with the different non-verbal behavioral cues pinpointed through their study in order to better recognize displays of anxiety and offer constructive and timely support (p. 131).

From simplicity to complexity 19

Connections with other dimensions of psychology

In addition to this dynamic turn, concurring with my arguments that emotions ought not to be considered in isolation, a sprinkling of empirical work has begun probing connections with other psychological aspects. In light of the often seemingly blended nature of emotions and motivations, MacIntyre and Vincze (2017) conducted a survey regarding various L2 learning emotions and motivations with 182 Italian secondary school learners studying German. The researchers found that pleasant emotions were more often reported and strongly correlated with motivation. In particular, (i) amusement significantly predicted confidence, frequency and quality of contact, effort, ideal L2 self (Dörnyei, 2009), and language anxiety (negatively correlated); (ii) lower levels of anger predicted more frequent and pleasant social contact, confidence and competence, and the ideal L2 self; and (iii) feeling peaceful predicted competence, confidence, and low anxiety (MacIntyre & Vincze, 2017).

In a more situated, classroom study, Méndez López and Peña Aguilar (2013) also delved into the connections between emotions and motivations for 18 undergraduate EFL students in Mexico. Data were gathered across one term via three different, qualitative tools: personal narratives written at the start of the study, emotional reaction journals kept over the 12 weeks of the term, and semi-structured interviews at the conclusion of data collection. Importantly, and counter to the findings of MacIntyre and Vincze's (2017) larger-scale study, the situated analysis elicited broad themes illuminating the motivationally ambivalent impact of emotions. On the one hand, pleasant emotions such as a sense of achievement or pride when praised often connected with greater self-efficacy and motivation to take risks in L2 study; on the other hand, almost all (16 of 18) of the participants agreed that "after a positive emotion there was nothing to do but enjoy the feeling", meaning that in terms of motivation, "they did nothing to improve their language learning" (Méndez López & Peña Aguilar, 2013, p. 117). In turn, unpleasant emotions, such as anxiety linked with assessment and feedback led some students to lose motivation to continue the course, while perceptions of inferiority to classmates prompted some to reduce their effort in class. Another key finding, however, was that unpleasant emotions could, at times, provide learners with a "way of understanding what they were doing wrong and how to improve on that particular skill", such that "students embraced negative emotions as learning opportunities" (Méndez López & Peña Aguilar, 2013, p. 118).

Rather than setting out to examine connections between emotions and a specific psychological element, such intersections emerged naturally in one of my own studies (Sampson, 2019b). The analysis itself was an extension of Sampson (2020 – see earlier in this chapter), in which reflective journals, as part of action research, had unearthed the diversity of my learners' feelings. Although the findings in Sampson (2020) included tentative connections between feelings and references to their object foci, the analysis seemed too simplistic and static (Morin, 2008). Hence, I decided to draw on the complexity property of interwoven and parallel timescales (see, e.g., de Bot, 2015) to conduct a reanalysis. I overtly coded object foci by timescales which made sense for the educational context, such as activity, lesson, lesson series, and semester or life. I then used egocentric coding comparison tables for each participant to organize the object foci into timescales as rows and study weeks as columns. I also incorporated relevant peer-perspectives into the coding comparison tables. This "timescales analysis" (Sampson, 2021) revealed that my students' interpretations of their emotional experiences were founded in bidirectional sensemaking emergent from the here-and-now and life experiences transported into the learning context. Longer timescales of learner psychology, such as understandings of personality, identity, beliefs and motivation, colored feelings in the classroom, while felt, social experiences in the classroom also impacted these longer timescales. Hence, I argued that researchers should take care to not conceive of emotions as purely "momentary" responses to stimuli but that they are grounded in ongoing sensemaking.

Returning to the specific emotion of anxiety, two studies from a volume edited by Gkonou et al. (2017) also provide illustrations of the usefulness of taking a more holistic perspective. In the first of these, Simsek and Dörnyei (2017) applied McAdams and Pals' (2006) proposition of intersecting tiers of personality to understand what they term "the anxious self" for some L2 learners. Data collection involved a combination of quantitative means to narrow down cases of interest and resulting qualitative interviews with the selected 16 highly anxious Turkish university students in EFL classes. These researchers found that some learners "described their anxious manifestations in L2 performance as if those were the outworking of a fairly independent dimension of their overall self" (Simsek & Dörnyei, 2017, p. 55). However, a closer look at the data also showed an interplay between general anxiety at a dispositional trait level of personality, anxiety with characteristic adaptations in the specific situation of L2 learning, and the ways in which participants narrated understandings of their experiences into their ongoing identities. Simsek and Dörnyei (2017) were particularly drawn to the differences in such "integrative life narratives" (McAdams & Pals, 2006) described by students, concluding that:

> Adding a narrative component to our understanding of language anxiety has practical implications. Learner stories can be *re-narrated*, which

in turn can affect the whole tenor of the anxious self, and appropriate "redemptive" strategies might be able to turn any negative trajectories into more positive ones.

(p. 66 – emphasis in original)

In an application of ideas from Bronfenbrenner (1979) and Kramsch (2002), Gkonou (2017), instead, attempted to understand language anxiety through an ecological systems approach. The research involved seven adult Greek EFL learners at an intermediate proficiency level, enrolled at private language schools. These participants were selected on the basis of being highly anxious through analysis of their scores on the Foreign Language Classroom Anxiety Scale (Horwitz et al., 1986). The learners kept weekly diaries over a 3-month period and participated in a semi-structured interview one week after the end of the diary writing. Gkonou's analysis showed interactions between nested "levels":

- The microsystem of experiences in EFL classrooms, predominantly through speaking anxiety linked to peer pressure, competitiveness, fear of derision for mistakes, and social comparisons of effort and ability.
- The mesosystem of participants' past learning experiences, revolving around memories of anxiety emergent from their former EFL teachers' own anxiety and condescending behaviors, perceptions of failure on tests, and past interpersonal interactions.
- The combined exosystem and macrosystem of local (rural, Greek) beliefs about foreign language education, in which teacher expectations of success (often measured through attainment of certificates) and a shared realization that English is necessary for professional advancement added constant pressure to students' studies (Gkonou, 2017, pp. 142–149).

Gkonou's (2017) experiences through the research led her to argue that "the fact that the microsystem is strongly influenced by the remaining three ecosystems and that there is a complex and dynamic interplay among all four ecosystems" means "delimiting the notion of context to the microsystem only would be a shortcoming for research and teaching" (p. 151).

Situated case studies

Such studies make critical headway into exploring the interrelationships between a variety of psychological dimensions and emotions in L2 learning. However, as MacIntyre and Vincze (2017) underline, in much of the other past research (predominantly of a quantitative nature), "it is not known to what extent emotions experienced by individuals ... mirror the group-level patterns reported" (p. 82). There has, however, been some (though, I would argue, not nearly enough) fascinating research taking a fine angle on individual or group cases.

One such study is that reported by Garrett and Young (2009). This research included analysis of data collected through twice-weekly informal interviews as the first author (Garrett – a teacher of French) participated in an intensive Brazilian-Portuguese university course for 8 weeks. Analysis unveiled that Garrett's affective responses emerged in interaction with four object foci over the course. First, although the smallest number of responses, interest related very strongly to encountering new aspects of Portuguese and Brazilian culture. Second, Garrett's identity as a fellow teacher (of L2 French) connected with positive emotional evaluations of the teaching styles of her instructors and materials. Third, comparisons between knowledge of other languages (in which she was more fluent) and the target language also linked with emotions. Garrett remarked upon approximately two-thirds more unpleasant emotions in this regard, as she felt overwhelmed, especially during speaking activities. Finally, the most frequently occurring theme concerned social relations with peers and instructors, which witnessed ambivalent emotions. Dynamicity was especially evident here: Although Garrett initially felt insecure based on negative social comparisons of ability and conflicts with her identity as a more fluent speaker of other languages, as time passed, these same social comparisons prompted a realization that, in fact, all students were finding the course challenging.

In contrast to this truly individual, contextualized approach, Imai (2010) instead offers a refreshing vision of the ways in which emotions (co-)emerge in groups. The study centered on the interactions of three Japanese undergraduates during collaborative preparation toward a group presentation for their EFL class. Data collection, thus, occurred in sessions outside of regular lesson time via three focused tools: video recording of the preparation discussions (in Japanese), emotion logs and questionnaires, and participants' own interpretations of the discussions through stimulated recall (Gass & Mackey, 2000). A specific episode in one of these discussions formed the focus of the presented analysis, drawing on Denzin's (1984) proposition of "emotional intersubjectivity" shared across people in social settings. During the event of concern, initial understandings of the pedagogical task espoused by the three students were adapted via emotional intersubjectivities grounded in verbal cues. Through a detailed analysis principally focused on the discourse of the discussion, Imai illustrates the way in which these co-formed, emotional understandings prompted group members to renegotiate their goal for the presentation and disregard the teacher-intended pedagogical outcome. In reflecting on one of the few studies of L2 emotions to take a truly social perspective, Imai (2010) concludes that there is a need to consider "emotions as socially and discursively constructed acts of communication that mediate learning and development" (p. 288). The L2 study emotion agenda, thus, ought to recognize that:

> What gives real significance to a language learner's own learning is not just a particular *meaning* that the researcher assigns to a specific type of emotion a priori, such as language anxiety and willingness to communicate, but the *sense* that each learner interactively constructs, negotiates, and appropriates regarding an emotional experience.
>
> (Imai, 2010, p. 288 – emphasis in original)

A final study that uncovers much of the need for situated research into L2 study emotions is one that I conducted as an extension of Sampson and Yoshida (2021; see also earlier in this chapter). As the reader may remember, this research involved undergraduate EFL students in Japan and their JFL peers in Australia in the context of an online L2 text-chat exchange. The study had collected introspective reflections and text-chat dialogical data to explore perceptions of feelings over seven chat sessions. Although Sampson and Yoshida (2021) had presented a wide-tooth analysis of the general detail, range, and foci to the feelings that learners had experienced during the chat exchange, we became curious about the emotional trajectories of certain of the chat dyads. Out of a total of 21 pairs in Sampson and Yoshida (2020), we used a narrative approach to center on the feeling trajectories of one particular chat dyad. We chose this pair because their feelings across sessions appeared to be an outlier from the experiences of other participants – while most dyads had reflected similar, pleasant emotional paths across the course of the chat exchange, the members of this dyad had markedly divergent experiences. The combination of data in a narrative form uniquely illuminated the emergence of the participants' varied emotional trajectories over time. The introspective data – students' reflections on each chat session – allowed glimpses of their emotional sensemaking from (sometimes mistaken) perceptions of seemingly trivial occurrences that were evident in the dialogic data – the chat transcripts of participants. The findings showed that the individual chatters' feelings were heavily impacted by their interactions in the particular social context, with the social context in turn co-formed via their perceptions of each other and other ongoing psychological processes (Sampson & Yoshida, 2020).

Conclusion

Recollecting the résumé of tasks denoted by Arnold and Brown (1999), Pavlenko (2013), and Dewaele (2021) described earlier, the empirical work in this chapter provides various exemplars of how we might strengthen

Table 2.1 Contributions of recent L2 study emotion research

	Dewaele & MacIntyre (2016) (enjoyment & anxiety)	Pawlak, Kruk, et al. (2020) (boredom object foci)	Pawlak, Zawodniak, et al. (2020b) (boredom trajectories)	Sampson (2020) (variety of classroom emotions)	Sampson & Yoshida (2021) (variety of online emotions)	Gregersen et al. (2017) (idiodynamic study)	MacIntyre & Vincze (2017) (motivation & emotions)	Méndez López & Peña Aguilar (2013) (motivation & emotions)	Sampson (2019) (emotional emergence over timescales)	Simsek & Dörnyei (2017) (personality & emotions)	Gkonou (2017) (ecological anxiety)	Garrett & Young (2009) (individual case study)	Imai (2010) (group case study)	Sampson & Yoshida (2020) (narrative of a chat dyad)
Arnold & Brown (1999)														
Problems created by negative emotions	o	o				o								
Potential of positive emotions	o			o	o		o			o		o	o	o
More concern with emotional natures and needs		o		o	o					o			o	o
Pavlenko (2013)														
Need to move focus away from purely anxiety	o	o		o	o		o	o	o	o			o	o
Need to focus on social nature of emotions	o					o			o		o	o	o	o
Dewaele (2021)														
Methods to "capture" emotions unequivocally		o		o	o				o	o			o	o
'Intermeshing of emotions with other aspects	o	o		o	o	o	o	o		o		o	o	o
Pertinent timescales		o o							o o		o o			
Dynamic qualities of emotions	o	o		o	o	o	o	o		o	o	o	o	o

[1] Note: Although Dewaele (2021) originally remarked upon the challenges of "disentangling" emotions from other aspects of L2 development, research rather seems to be more understanding of the interrelated nature of emotions with other aspects of L2 learners' psychologies and lives.

research into L2 study emotions. Table 2.1 summarizes my interpretations of such contributions. The studies upon which I have primarily focused throughout this chapter are listed horizontally, while the research tasks are placed vertically. At a glance, it ought to be apparent that many of the identified hopes for, and challenges to, conducting research into L2 study emotions are being answered by contemporary empirical work. Nevertheless, gaps remain, in particular with regard to explorations of the social context of emotions, ways to more sufficiently capture emotionality, and consideration of appropriate timescales upon which to focus. Indeed, there remain appeals for a plurality of research methods to explore the dynamicity of language learners' psychologies more generally (MacIntyre et al., 2015, 2021; Prior, 2019; Sampson & Pinner, 2021; Ushioda, 2009) and emotions specifically (Dewaele & Li, 2020), as well as a push for smaller scale, emic research by classroom practitioners in cooperation with learners rather than "researchers-as-outsiders" (Ushioda, 2020).

It is in the context of such calls that the following chapters set forth the tools with which I am working in order to gain contextualized, dynamic insights to the social emergence of the emotions of learners in my own L2 classes.

3 Interactions between the whole and parts in the emergence of L2 study feelings

Those working in education contexts maintain a constantly shifting focus at one and the same time upon individuals, pairs, small groups, as well as a class as a whole. This concern is one of the unique requirements of education, much more so than other "helping" professions such as nursing and social work (Urdan, 2014). Day in and day out, teachers take all these social groupings into account and make dynamic adaptations based on their fluid observations. Yet, it is naturally not only teachers who continually update their understandings of the interactions within the classroom. With the diverse array of people making up a class group on any day, students also quickly gain an implicit sense of the overall (emotional) atmosphere, or the buildup over time of particular "class climates". As Nitta and Nakata (2021) explain, "class climate is analogous to geographical climate; that is, a number of factors interact to create a group feeling and atmosphere, which affects people's desire to engage in certain activities" (p. 175). From a complexity perspective, class climate is a classic example of self-organized emergence: What the members of a class group "bring into" the classroom and the ways in which they (emotionally) interact coalesce to form class climate (the parts engender an emergent whole), yet at the same time, this class climate affords and constrains certain forms of behavior and emotions (the whole engenders the emergent parts). There is circular causality (Witherington, 2011). In terms of the focus of this book, the emotionality of the individuals and the overall group self-organizes rather than being directed purely by any one governing agent or trigger.

The current chapter, thus, begins the empirical section of the book by exploring the interactions between the whole and the parts from a number of different angles. I commence by providing a short, narrative overview of the background and implementation of the research. Following, the chapter turns to a description of general trends to feelings[1] across the participants, and a look at how the feelings connected with different segments of each lesson. Finally, I describe the way in which I utilized a diagrammatical

Interactions between the whole and parts 27

tool known as multiple threading (Davis & Sumara, 2006) in order to more adequately preserve a focus on individual learners and the class group as a whole.

Instigating research

As a classroom teacher of compulsory EFL courses for Japanese undergraduates, it has been my observation that learners seem to emotionally connect to differing degrees with various activities in my lessons – no doubt a sense shared by many practitioners around the world. Of specific note, one of my courses with a focus on developing students' listening skills offers a great degree of freedom in implementation of learning tasks. While it employs a textbook set by the university as part of a coordinated curriculum, textbook exercises amount for at most half of the lesson content. In extension to the listening focus, individual class teachers are encouraged to introduce additional speaking activities. I had previously engaged in action research exploring motivational aspects of speaking activities based on Dörnyei's (2009) L2 Motivational Self System (e.g., Sampson, 2017, 2018, 2019a). Yet, throughout such action research, I also became aware that, perhaps even more so than reflecting on their motivation, my learners were very conscious of and eloquent in expressing understandings of their emotions during lessons (e.g., Sampson, 2019b, 2020). Hence, I wanted to take a closer look at how the emotions of my learners evolved in connection with different dimensions of their lessons with me.

One class of Japanese undergraduates (n = 28) agreed to contribute data for the study that forms the basis of this book. These students were first-year science and technology majors at a small university north of Tokyo. Participants consisted of six female and 22 male learners who were all Japanese nationals. The group had an average age of 19 years – the majority of students (23) were 19 years old, while five students turned 20 over the course of the semester. Participants' English levels ranged from around elementary to intermediate on the Common European Framework of Reference for Language (Council of Europe, 2001) – their Test of English for International Communication (TOEIC) listening/reading scores averaged 518 (minimum 370, maximum 620, standard deviation 71). Considering their overseas experiences related to the focal language, ten learners had visited English-speaking countries for travel, yet none for extended living experiences. Prior to entering the university, all the participants had attended public schools in Japan at which they began formal EFL study from junior-high school (12 to 13 years old). To this end, they had 6 years of formal study before entering university.

28 *Interactions between the whole and parts*

All participants were members of the same class, studying a compulsory EFL listening/speaking course. The course ran for one semester, consisting of 14 weeks of one, 90-minute lesson per week. I conducted the lessons in a communicative fashion, with a mix of skill-based exercises from the set listening textbook alongside interactive discussions and tasks. In the interest of allowing opportunities for the first-year undergraduates to encounter different ideas and develop varied friendship groups, students were randomly allotted to work together for two to three lessons then reassigned to new groups.

Data collection

In the compulsory curriculum, students were required to reflect on their EFL lessons. A rationale delivered to learners about such reflection was based on Dewey's (1916/1944) contention that it is the process of thinking back on experiences from which we can truly learn and develop. Drawing on Rodgers (2002), the explanation also included a description of reflection as a systematic, rigorous, disciplined way of thinking, involving stages of experiencing, describing experience, distancing and analysis of experience, and subsequent intelligent action based on these deeper understandings. Accordingly, learners had to submit a reflective journal entry after each lesson, with the specific focus of writing defined by individual classroom teachers. Thus, although data for the study were collected from multiple angles, analysis in this chapter draws purely on these reflective journals.

As a form of introspective data collection, cautions have been sounded about journals because of the investment of time required by participants (Rose, 2020). Yet, as journal-writing was part of the compulsory course anyway, I judged that this method of gaining insight would not overburden participants nor overly interrupt regular classroom action. I thus decided to ask my students whether I might use their reflections as data to allow me to learn more about their L2 study emotions. Indeed, journals in classroom research have been praised for their potential to "take us to a place that no other data collection method can reach – into the mind of the learner or teacher" (Nunan & Bailey, 2009, p. 307). Journals have the capacity to furnish contextualized, dynamic, personal, and candid perceptions of learning experiences (Gilmore, 2016; Nunan & Bailey, 2009; Sampson, 2016a). While providing participants with a degree of agency to proffer their own thoughts and interpretations as data, journals are also efficacious in allowing systematic insights into the dynamicity of phenomena over time (Rose, 2020). Stressing the benefits of journals for classroom research, Phelps (2005) additionally remarks that:

No-one knows the complex interplay of factors that impact on an individual, or the significance of any one factor, greater than the individual themselves. This is not to assume for a moment that the individual learner is fully aware of all these factors, but rather that they are in a better position to understand them than anyone else.

(p. 40)

In line with the university policy, the journal was introduced as a reflective pedagogical task, with a brief rationale of the benefits of reflection provided in Japanese. After different lesson segments, learners were encouraged to take notes about their perceptions of feelings and then collate them as a reflective journal entry. Intending to reduce the potential quandary of a large variation in the length of reflections, part of assessment was based on how many entries students submitted and whether these texts were more than a minimum of 100 words. To facilitate the journaling process, as well as reduce problems of recall (Hall, 2008; Nunan & Bailey, 2009; Porto, 2007), participants submitted the journals as an email to me directly following each lesson. The prompt was:

> This semester, please write reflections about your feelings connected to experiences in lessons. After each activity, take some notes. Do not only list the activities we did in the lesson – you should write about your feelings connected with participating in that activity. Then, after each lesson, use your notes to write a reflective journal entry of at least 100 words in English. Send your journal entry as an email to Richard by 23:59 on the day of our lesson.

As one may notice, I asked my learners to write in their second language, English. Certainly, utilizing journal data collected in the L2 has been criticized, as participants' capacity to write what they truly think is determined by their level of L2 capability (Hall, 2008). However, I judged the English level of learners in this context to be reasonable based on their initial English test scores. As the journaling was included as part of pedagogical practice, I moreover wanted to show my respect for participants' developing L2 identities (Sampson, 2016a). Learners were, therefore, encouraged and wrote these journals in English, although they did occasionally use some Japanese phrases. Entries were collected for 13 of 14 lessons across the semester (I had to cancel one lesson in the eighth week due to attendance at an academic conference overseas). The data collected via learner journals amounted to 343 entries (an average of 26 per lesson), with a total corpus of just over 38,000 words.

In parallel, I kept a journal of my teaching experiences over the semester. I intended this teacher journal to add further context and a different perspective to the data collected from students. At times, I was able to take brief notes during class of any incidents or behaviors by students that particularly caught my attention, though this was certainly not a consistent practice. Luckily, I did not have any other engagements directly following the lessons each week and could write immediately after my experiences with this class. As a result, my reflections mainly focused on impressions during the lessons. I also, however, included occasional reflections after having read the emailed journal entries from learners, as well as some pondering on the research process itself. The teacher journal ended up with entries regarding all 13 lessons and totaled a little over 11,000 words.

Feelings with a broad brush

I initially conducted a content analysis following Saldana (2016) of learners' reflective journals using the qualitative data management software NVivo. I started by looking at the collected data and recognizing without predetermined categories one of the basic elements of emotions – the subjective feelings upon which students reflected. New codes were created whenever a phenomenon in participant entries was found not to be represented by the existing codes. I employed overlapping codes, meaning that a section of data could have multiple codes to facilitate exploration of patterns of connection between themes at a later date (Bazeley, 2013). This means that an instance might be coded to two or more feelings. Entries were also coded to the segment of lessons to which they referred, and a "week" code to enable examination of dynamics within lessons and across the semester.

At times, participants directly referenced certain feelings. At other times, I drew on my own past experiences with research into L2 study emotions and in lessons to code implied feelings. In this task, my teacher journal provided insightful context as a reminder of the activities students were engaged in during each lesson. It additionally allowed me to recollect certain incidents that furnished emotional background to learners' writing. After a first pass through the journals, I then delved into the data coded to each feeling. I shifted references to other codes when I deemed them to represent the emotions of learners more appropriately. With the relatively large amount of journal text, this revision was especially important for data that had been coded early on, in pursuance of maintaining consistency across the analysis. This stage of analysis, therefore, comprised a quantifying of qualitative data (Onwuegbuzie & Daniel, 2003) to gain a sense of the diversity of feelings and the degree of their experience.

Table 3.1 displays the various feelings, their working definitions emergent from analysis, and examples of coding for each.

The range of feelings evident in Table 3.1 aligns, to a large degree, with the findings of my own past research unearthing the vivid variety of L2 study emotions in classroom settings (Sampson, 2020). That said, there are some additions: First, the reader might be surprised at the inclusion of two forms of motivation (usually divorced from other emotional aspects, particularly in past L2 research). However, I concur with Lemke (2013) in proposing that motivation is certainly a feeling that we can perceive, and as such, it makes little sense to divorce it from other feelings. Some other feelings not found in Sampson (2020), such as relief and empathy/sympathy, were more often than not tied to particular temporal events in the lessons in this specific semester (for instance, after worrying about their new teacher for the semester – me! – learners especially mentioned relief after the first lesson). Another notable addition is that of the concept of relatedness, a feeling of social affirmation and connection with others (Ryan & Deci, 2002). This especially is one of the feelings that will be explored in more contextualized detail in the chapters to come.

Considering the recent expansion of interest in L2 study boredom (Pawlak et al., 2020a–c – see also Chapter 2), references to this feeling are conspicuously absent. In light of the fact that participants in my study reflected on a diverse range of other feelings, one might come to the conclusion that boredom is not widespread. Alternatively, it could be surmised that my lessons were so engaging for students that boredom was not on their emotional radars. While, as a classroom practitioner, I would certainly like to believe the latter, the more likely explanation relates to the specific form of data. Because of the nature of reflective journals and the unavoidable condition, as a dimension of the compulsory assessed items for the course, that students would be conscious of me reading their entries, they may have been biased in what they included. It is certainly even possible that they may have written about boredom while taking their in-lesson notes but excluded such ponderings when submitting their eventual reflection by email. I must admit that I cannot refute the potential for such a bias. However, I would also stress that complexity perspectives understand the observer as part of the observed. As Davis and Sumara (2006) remind:

> Complexity thinking compels researchers to consider how they are implicated in the phenomena that they study – and, more broadly, to acknowledge that their descriptions of the world exist in complex (i.e., nested, co-implicated, ambiguously bounded, dynamic, etc.) relationship with the world.
>
> (p. 15)

Table 3.1 Feelings, working definitions, and examples of coding to each

Feeling	Working definitions	Example coding
Anticipation	Feeling pleasure toward an expected future event	I look forward to next class, new partner, and new Lego; I hope next class will be enjoyable, too.
Anxiety	Feeling worried about something that is happening or might happen in the future	I was nervous before the class; I was worried about talking to other students.
Being impressed	Feeling admiration or respect for the actions of another	He was very good at speaking English; Other members is so quick to build.
Disappointment	Feeling unhappy from the failure of something hoped for or expected to happen	I tried something, but I couldn't do it. When this class finished, I regretted it very much.
Empathy/Sympathy	A feeling of experiencing or understanding another's feelings	I cannot talk with unknown people. So I sympathized teacher.
Enjoyment	Feeling pleasure caused by doing or experiencing something one likes	I enjoyed talking with him; I have a good time, learning English.
Excitement	Feeling heightened energy, enthusiasm and eagerness	I was so excited this activity; I was excited to communicate with many classmates.
Gratitude	Feeling appreciation to someone for their actions	He knew songs of my favorite artist so I was very happy. She was kind, so I could relax.
Interest	A feeling that accompanies or causes special attention to something	I had an interest in a student who are different major with me. Personality activity was interesting.
Motivation in lesson	Feeling a want to act in the lesson (engagement)	I positively expressed myself; I spoke more than last class.
Motivation in future	Feeling a want to act in the future	I thought I need to achieve my conversation skill. Next lessons, I want to talk with my friends more smoothly.
Progress/Sense of achievement	A proud feeling of having improved or done something difficult with effort	I was happy to be able to complete it; I think I can speak English more today, I'm so glad.
Relatedness	Feeling connected with and affirmed by others	I talked about cooking and listening to music, and I was glad that she know about my favorite singer!

(*Continued*)

Table 3.1 Continued

Feeling	Working definitions	Example coding
Relief	A feeling of release from expected anxiety or stress	I felt you are kind and friendly. So, I was able to calm down.
Sense of difficulty	Feeling something is hard to do, or less confident because one cannot achieve what one wants	There are so many words that sound alike but have different meanings, so it is difficult for me to distinguish.
Surprise	A feeling caused by something unexpected happening	To my surprise, other students talked to me with confidence; I'm so astonished.

In recognizing that I myself am part of the research process, it goes without saying that the motives of students and the data that they produced will have been influenced through their perceptions of my role as the class teacher (McNiff & Whitehead, 2011). However, I also do feel that the relationships I was able to build with learners over the semester encouraged a sense of trust. I can also say that participants were reminded throughout that the assessment of their journal entries was not based on the details of the content per se, but rather on how many entries they submitted over the required length. Nevertheless, I have little doubt that learners would have experienced boredom at some point, yet this is not reflected in the journal data.

Moving on to a little more detail of the ways in which these feelings were represented across the population, Table 3.2 includes the percentage of student journal entries in which specific feelings occurred, the spread of students who mentioned any particular feeling at least once in their journals, and commonly co-occurring feelings.

I will not overly discuss the fine particularities of these results here, as my primary purpose in this book is to focus in a more situated manner on the dynamic, social emergence of emotions – something about which these numbers, while interesting to a degree, can offer little insight. Notwithstanding, some interpretation is certainly called for.

A point of note with which to begin is the ranking of anxiety – being only the ninth most-remarked upon feeling by participants, one may indeed wonder why so much past empirical attention has been devoted to its experience (Pavlenko, 2013). While 93% of students did mention it at some time in their journals, other traditionally "unpleasant" feelings such as disappointment (48% of entries, ranked sixth, noted by 100% of students) or a sense of difficulty (81% of entries, ranked second, noted by 100% of students)

Table 3.2 Degree of occurrence of feelings across learner journals, percentage of students mentioning feelings, and feelings co-occurring

Feeling	Percentage of entries (rank)	Percentage of students	Commonly co-occurring feelings
Anticipation	14% (13)	64%	Progress/Sense of achievement; enjoyment
Anxiety	25% (9)	93%	Progress/Sense of achievement; motivation in future
Being impressed	21% (12)	82%	Interest; gratitude
Disappointment	48% (6)	100%	Motivation in future; progress/sense of achievement
Empathy/Sympathy	6% (16)	46%	Enjoyment; interest
Enjoyment	61% (5)	100%	Progress/Sense of achievement; sense of difficulty
Excitement	10% (15)	54%	Progress/Sense of achievement; interest
Gratitude	31% (7)	93%	Progress/Sense of achievement; sense of difficulty
Interest	61% (4)	100%	Enjoyment; sense of difficulty
Motivation in lesson	30% (8)	86%	Progress/Sense of achievement; disappointment
Motivation in future	63% (3)	100%	Sense of difficulty; disappointment
Progress/Sense of achievement	94% (1)	96%	Sense of difficulty; enjoyment
Relatedness	24% (10)	96%	Enjoyment; interest
Relief	12% (14)	64%	Anxiety; progress/sense of achievement
Sense of difficulty	81% (2)	100%	Motivation in future; progress/sense of achievement
Surprise	22% (11)	93%	Interest; relatedness

outweigh anxiety. Such findings are again congruent with my past research (Sampson, 2020; Sampson & Yoshida, 2021).

"Pleasant" experiences of enjoyment (61% of entries, ranked fifth, noted by 100% of students), interest (61% of entries, ranked fourth, noted by 100% of students), and progress or a sense of achievement (94% of entries, ranked first, noted by 96% of learners) were more prevalent in my lessons. Such findings support the proliferation of explorations of positive psychology in L2 learning (MacIntyre et al., 2016; Oxford, 2016), investigation of enjoyment (Boudreau et al., 2018; Dewaele & Alfawzan, 2018; Dewaele & MacIntyre, 2014, 2016), and Dörnyei and Ushioda's (2011) – largely unanswered – call for research into the interactions between interest and other dimensions of L2 psychology such as motivation.

Perhaps, also significantly, this first, broad-brush sweep through the data reveals a contrast in commonly co-occurring feelings between the pleasant and unpleasant. On the one hand, as discussed in the previous chapter, MacIntyre and Vincze (2017) have found that pleasant emotions more commonly correlate with motivation toward L2 study. On the other hand, Méndez López and Peña Aguilar's (2013) classroom-based research revealed that the opposite was also possible – their participants remarked upon motivation emergent from experiences of difficulty, whereas success and enjoyment, at times, connected with apathy (pp. 117–118). Even a cursory look at Table 3.2 suggests data from learners in the current study matches with these latter findings. Participants more often mentioned motivation to act in the future in the context of a sense of difficulty, disappointment, and anxiety. In contrast, "pleasant" feelings such as a sense of progress and achievement, enjoyment and interest were not connected with motivation to the same degree. Unlike Méndez López and Peña Aguilar's (2013) study, my research, unfortunately, did not follow up with students to ask in detail about such relationships, although they will become apparent in later chapters taking a more focused approach. It might be hypothesized, however, that the differences between MacIntyre and Vincze's (2017) larger-scale, survey-based approach and the smaller-scale, qualitative approaches applied by Méndez López and Peña Aguilar (2013) and myself in the present study could have played a role in these conflicting findings. It is also perhaps pertinent to note that the mere presence of references to the "want to action" (Dörnyei & Ushioda, 2011) of motivation does not necessarily equate with resultant action.

Feelings across a lesson

The area of additional language *motivation* research is advanced in its consideration of dynamics (e.g., Dörnyei et al., 2015). In doing so, many studies revolve around motivation over longer timescales such as semesters or years of study (e.g., Irie & Ryan, 2015; Nitta, 2013; Yashima & Arano, 2015). Regarding L2 study emotions, idiodynamic studies (e.g., Boudreau et al., 2018; Gregersen et al., 2014, 2017; MacIntyre, 2012) take a fine angle on second-by-second fluctuations. Another, shorter timescale, no doubt of interest to many teachers, is the way in which feelings interact with different activities, topics, and segments in a lesson. In the current study, lessons were demarcated into four broadly repeating elements for each session, which are displayed in Table 3.3.

36 Interactions between the whole and parts

Table 3.3 Lesson segments involved in the focal course

Usual order	Lesson segment	Description	Usual time allocated
1	Short conversation session	Pairs or small groups selected from a range of topic prompts to continue relatively free conversation	Between 2 (start of semester) to 8 minutes (end of semester)
2	Textbook exercises	Students worked individually or in pairs/groups on exercises in the set textbook, involving the development of listening strategies	Average of 30 to 40 minutes
3	Extra textbook activities	More interactive activities involving teacher-developed materials and which built on and extended the basic listening strategies	Average of 10 to 20 minutes
4	Humanistic/ reflective activities	A range of interactive activities based on humanistic education principles (Gill & Thomson, 2017)	Average of 25 to 30 minutes

As a first step to investigating the focus of learners' feelings, I wondered in what ways there were similarities and differences between their connections to these lesson segments. In parallel with searching for different feelings, during the initial analysis I had coded their context in terms of lesson segment. It was, therefore, a straightforward task to run a Boolean search in NVivo for the intersections between feelings and lesson segments across the semester. The results are displayed as stacked graphs in Figure 3.1.

A few notes are necessary. First, the graph of humanistic activities is skewed by the content of the opening lesson. Although there was a necessity for the usual "information transfer" of an introduction to the course, I also wanted to start the semester with a humanistic concern for "caring about connecting well with other people ... and to commit to friendships and relationships" (Gill & Thomson, 2017, p. 5). Hence, most activities on this day revolved around opportunities for learners to become more familiar with each other and me as the teacher. Similarly, the first occasion of the short conversation session appears, at first glance, to have witnessed a comparative outpouring of references to emotion. However, once again, the graph needs to be taken in some context – there were no additional textbook or humanistic activities on this day. Indeed, introduction of extra textbook activities was rather sporadic over the semester. A final note concerns lesson week eight – I remind the reader that the lesson was canceled because of my absence, with the result of a gap in the graphs.

Interactions between the whole and parts 37

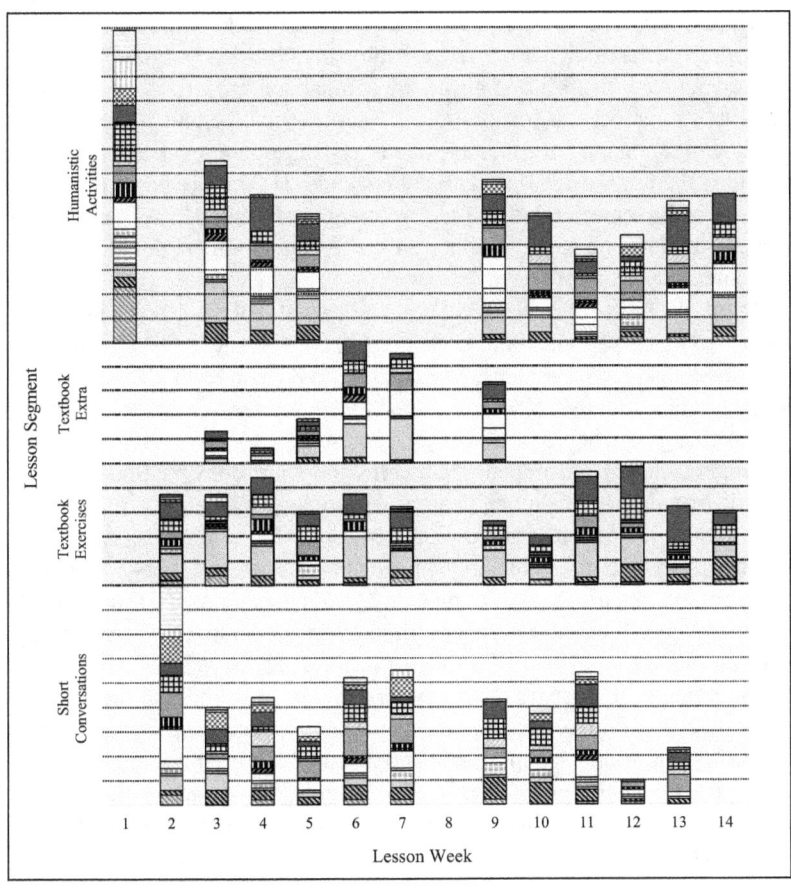

Figure 3.1 Compilation of number of references to feelings by lesson segment over the semester (the scale is by tens of references).

38 *Interactions between the whole and parts*

With these caveats in mind, the graphs in Figure 3.1 do, however, allow for some interesting comparisons across the lesson segments. While there are certainly drawbacks to dichotomizing emotions in a blanket fashion by valence (Oxford & Gkonou, 2021), an intriguing comparison can be made concerning the mix of references to "pleasant" and "unpleasant" feelings by lesson segment. Combining the three feelings of anxiety, disappointment, and a sense of difficulty, the textbook lesson segment engendered far more unpleasant feelings across the semester. Indeed, such references made up 38% of the feelings connected with time spent working on the textbook, almost double those in the context of the short conversations (21%) or humanistic activities (22%). That said, the most-referenced feelings for three of the lesson segments were, rather surprisingly, unpleasant: short conversation sessions (disappointment, 12%), textbook exercises (sense of difficulty, 25%), and textbook extra activities (sense of difficulty, 26%). In contrast, the humanistic activities connected most with enjoyment (15%) across the semester.

Another curious discrepancy concerns the short conversation sessions. Set side by side with the other, generally more lengthy elements of each lesson, short conversation sessions lasted between 2 to 8 minutes. Yet, immediately apparent is the ostensibly lopsided reference to feelings related to the short conversations. While, on average, they accounted for a mere 5% of lesson time, feelings references situated in the short conversation segment amounted to 27% of the overall total (even more astounding when noticing that there were no short conversation sessions in both the first and final lessons). As I have repeatedly mentioned, my purpose in this book is to consider emotions in a more situated, social fashion. It was this puzzling realization about the *quantitatively* large emotional impact of such a brief lesson segment that pushed me to explore in more detail the *qualitative* emergence of emotions through my learners' interactions connected with the short conversation sessions (see the following four chapters).

Focusing on individuals and group

The kinds of representations of analysis set out in the previous sections average across the individuals making up a class group. They afford us with a rather general impression of the emotionality of L2 students. As I remarked at the commencement of this chapter, however, educational contexts are somewhat unique in the way in which the people making up these social groups focus on individuals and the group at the same time. With a view to visualizing such diversity and degree of feelings over time for all learners and the class as a whole, I employed a representative strategy known as multiple threading (Davis & Sumara, 2006). Multiple threading "involves the presentation of several narrative strands" in which "some may

Interactions between the whole and parts 39

be only brief phrases or single images that punctuate the text, and strands may overlap or interlink at times" (Davis & Sumara, 2006, p. 162). As originally applied, these researchers illustrated how often and to what degree individual voices or ideas enrich an overall text, such as a research paper or dramatic performance. An adapted example is offered in Figure 3.2.

I have previously used multiple threading as a way of diagrammatizing such phenomena as the interactions between teacher and student affect (Sampson, 2016b); the gradual, self-organizing spread of learner motivation in a classroom setting (Sampson, 2016a); and the endeavors by students to act on images of "ideal classmates" (Sampson, 2018; see also Murphey et al., 2014 for theorizing of this fascinating concept). In the current study, in like fashion to some of my other work with emotions (Sampson, 2020, 2021; Sampson & Yoshida, 2021), through a reimagining of multiple threading, I visually represented not only how often but also in what ways specific students contributed to the overall "emotional narrative" or classroom climate (Nitta & Nakata, 2021) on any specific day and over time. The feelings multiple threading used lessons across the horizontal axis and individual learners down the vertical axis. I assigned a "square" to each learner in the class for each week of study. Based on the initial content analysis, I located different feelings experienced by a learner for a particular period of time. I then divided the square at the junction of learner-week by the number of different feelings mentioned and applied shading to represent these feelings. Therefore, in Figure 3.3 each square represents the range of feelings mentioned by an individual learner over a lesson.

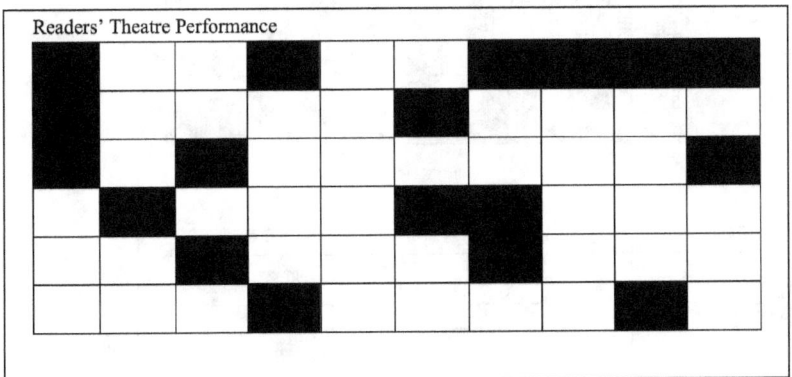

Figure 3.2 A multiple threading representation of a readers' theatre performance (adapted from Davis and Sumara [2006]). The horizontal axis is time, while the vertical axis is threads of discussion. Each horizontal row represents a thread of the discussion, with overlaps and recurrences.

40 *Interactions between the whole and parts*

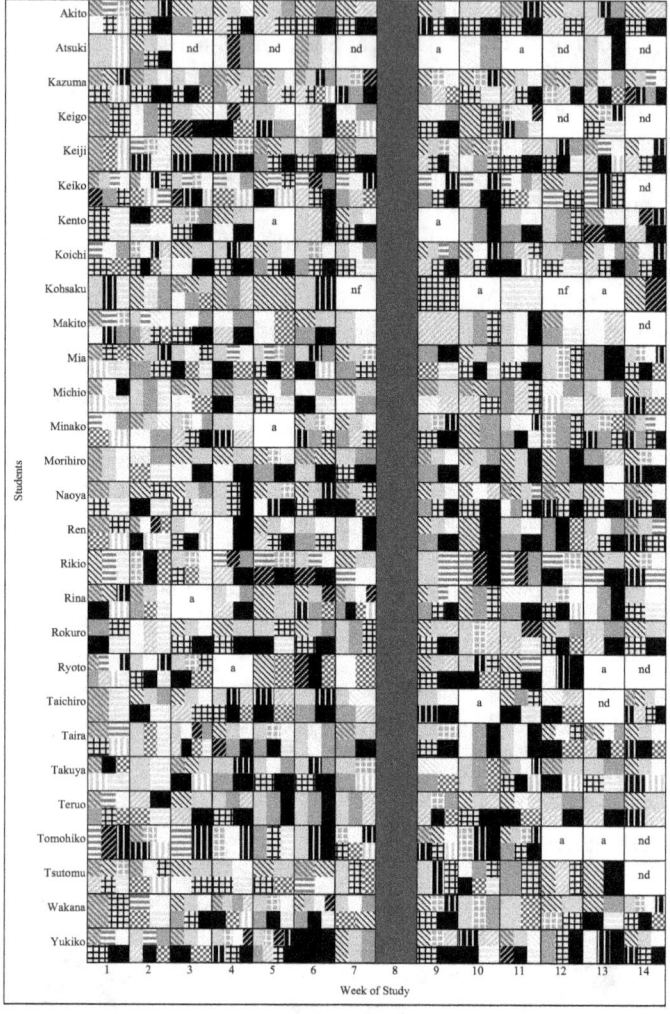

Figure 3.3 Feelings multiple threading for learners over the semester. Rows represent individual learners, while columns pertain to lessons. The different shading represents instances of different feelings mentioned in reflective journals for each lesson for that learner.

As the reader may no doubt feel when trying to take in the multiple threading with an entire class over a whole semester, this diagram presents rather a visual overload. Looked at this way, it asks for quite a deal of effort on the part of the observer. Nevertheless, I argue that multiple threading also offers, to a certain degree, more freedom of insight than might ordinarily be possible with many, more numerical representations of analyzed data. A multiple threading "*represents* (in the sense of calling something to mind, not in the sense of precise or fixed description) at the same time as it *presents* (that is, it opens up new interpretive possibilities)" (Davis & Sumara, 2006, p. 162 – emphasis in original). While a numerical summary, such as that presented in Table 3.2, gives us a very general idea of trends to feelings across the body of participants, the multiple threading allows us to maintain sight of the individual (student, feeling, lesson) and the whole (class group, feelings, lesson series or semester).

As teachers, we may tend to become overly focused on the content and quality of students' learning, their progress and achievement, their willingness to use the additional language, or lapse into silence (King & Smith, 2017; Smith & King, 2021; Yashima, 2002, 2021). Even though it might seem overwhelming at first, what I would, therefore, also urge is that a multiple threading reminds us of the kind of emotional landscape teachers and learners both encounter and co-create over every lesson in which we participate as a group. It prompts us to recognize the ever-present subplot of emotion that pervades learning spaces (although neuroscientific research shows us that emotions are certainly not playing "second fiddle" in anyone's learning processes; see Immordino-Yang, 2016; Immordino-Yang & Damasio, 2016). As researchers, the multiple threading technique admonishes us to do a more adequate job of considering the multiplicity of feelings in the L2 classroom. In congruence with Boudreau et al. (2018), the multiple threading furnishes an extremely visual reminder that there is a great deal of interpersonal variation in how feelings evolve over the course of classroom experiences. In so doing, it may also make us embarrassingly aware of how one-dimensional our past fixation on predominantly one affective factor – anxiety – has been (Pavlenko, 2013).

Naturally, the multiple threading is still an act in simplification. Yet, through multiple threading, we can look at any particular learner in different ways, such as gaining a sense of the diversity of their feelings in one particular lesson or tracing their feeling trajectory across a number of lessons. Moreover, it reminds us of the ways in which individual students all contribute to the whole of the emotional narrative or class climate (Nitta & Nakata, 2021): We can contrast the emotions of any selected students in the same class during a lesson or across time. At a glance, we can gain a sense of feelings for a particular lesson, perhaps nudging us to consider further what might have been occurring at that time to engender tendencies toward certain feelings across learners. Finally, we can also use the multiple threading matrix to observe the general emotional orientation of the class as a whole by looking at the complete picture.

Conclusion

In the current chapter, I aimed to provide some background in particular for the study that forms the basis of the following chapters. First, I described the classroom context and details of implementation of the study. Next, I set forth findings across participants unearthed via initial analysis. These findings revealed some general trends to the kinds of feelings my learners noted in the context of their L2 study. Moreover, I took a preliminary look at how these feelings connected with different segments of lessons as well as using a multiple threading representation (Davis & Sumara, 2006) to afford a detailed and holistic view of the feelings emergent in the class group. I argued that such a representation reminds us of the array of diverse colors making up the emotional fabric of a class at any point in time and over time.

It might seem odd to cast a chapter in which I have presented findings as "background". While useful to a degree, this nascent analysis does not illuminate the connections between learners' feelings and their focus. The analysis did, however, point to one segment of lessons that seemed to witness a disproportionately high degree of emotional writing by my learners. It was this recognition that prompted me to look back in more detail at the social emergence of emotions during the short conversation sessions.

Note

1 The focus in the current chapter is upon primarily the subjective perceptions of emotions about which learners were able to reflect in journals. The term "feelings" is, thus, employed (Damasio, 2003).

4 Focusing a small lens on experiential and discursive context

How do the emotions of the people in our classrooms evolve over the course of their interactions? As one way to interpret the social complexity of L2 learner psychology, Ushioda (2009) has suggested a "person-in-context relational view". While not specifically discussing emotions but, rather, emergent motivation, self, and identity, Ushioda (2009) encourages a focus on

- Real persons rather than learners as theoretical or averaged abstractions.
- The agency of these individual persons as thinking, feeling human beings (here, Ushioda refers to identities, personality, and motives, yet other aspects of a person's complex psychology, such as emotions, beliefs, and their unique history and background, are equally connoted).
- The interactions between such self-reflective agents and the system of social relations, activities, experiences, and contexts that they both form and through which they are formed (p. 220).

Ushioda's concern with "real persons" with unique psychologies aligns with the arguments of this book in taking a critical stance on research founded in simplicity: Oftentimes, past empirical work has dissociated the psychological focus of interest from other aspects of the day-to-day lives of research participants and cast them as purely "L2 learners". That is, Ushioda (2009) urges a consideration of the people in our learning spaces as rounded, particular human beings with numerous identities, only one of which may be their L2 identity. Through a person-in-context relational view, Ushioda (2015) advocates an overt appreciation of the complex interplay between various psychological elements, "comprising a dynamic constellation of cognitive, affective, motivational and behavioral characteristics in constant evolving interaction with one another" (p. 50). In light of such dynamics, the emotionality of learners may be impacted in unpredictable ways by any number of other aspects of their lives. Moreover, expressions of (or constraints on) psychological aspects do not occur in a vacuum. They are realized and refined through ongoing historical processes and interactions in a social context (Lemke, 2000; Prior, 2019). This social context is both formed and forming; there is a "mutually constitutive relationship between persons and the contexts in which they act" (Ushioda, 2009, p. 218). Put in the more general terms of complexity thinking, Larsen-Freeman and Cameron (2008) offer the idea of "co-adaptation", a "kind of mutual causality, in which change in one system leads to change in another system connected to it, and this mutual influencing continues over time" (p. 233). Such processes are clearly implicated in the sociality of learning spaces:

> We cannot ignore the integral part played by the individual learner in shaping context and in shaping the input generated within that context. What L2 learners say or do, or choose not to say or do, how they behave, what they think, how they respond to their context mentally, affectively, verbally, behaviorally, will all contribute in complex ways to shaping and changing the developing context.
> (Ushioda, 2011, p. 188)

Yet, remarkably few studies of L2 learner psychology take interpersonal interactions over time as their focus (Prior, 2019; Ushioda, 2009). Even in the review of neoteric empirical work discussed in Chapter 2, only Imai's (2010) study directly homes in on the co-construction of emotions through focusing on interpersonal communicative acts. This, despite the manifestly social environments in which L2 learning and use occurs, and in which learners express and develop their identities. As Denzin (1984) proposes, we might gain a good deal (not least in terms of the soundness of research interpretations) by "returning emotion ... to the world of interaction" (pp. 10–11). In so doing, researchers can work to more sufficiently ensure that "emotion's meanings, nuances, subtleties, innuendoes, distortions, and significations are brought to life and thickly described within the lived experiences of ordinary people" (Denzin, 1984, p. 11).

As expounded in Chapter 3, one of the most tantalizing findings from the initial analysis centered on the short conversation sessions in which groups or pairs chose different conversation prompts and continued increasingly longer conversations over the semester. Despite their relatively brief timeframe each week, this segment of lessons seemed emotionally charged for many learners. If, as Immordino-Yang (2016) contends, it is vital to "find ways to leverage the emotional aspects of learning in education" (p. 18), as a teacher, I was curious to take a more focused look at the development of emotions during these social interactions.

Investigating the interplay of the social with the experiential

Discursive psychology

One pertinent tool for unearthing the socially grounded emergence of L2 study emotions through language might be a form of discourse analysis known as discursive psychology (DP) (Edwards, 1997). As Wiggins (2017) describes, DP is "a theoretical and analytical approach to discourse which treats talk and text as an object of study in itself, and psychological concepts as socially managed and consequential in interaction" (p. 4). Through detailed, line-by-line analysis of interaction transcripts which include additional contextual information such as prosody, facial expressions, and particulars of the evolving situation, such approaches aim to demonstrate that interlocutors orient to some features of a conversation as emotional (Ruusuvuori, 2012). DP is strongly supported by recent research into emotional expression, with Keltner et al. (2019) noting that "facial expressions, vocalizations, patterns of bodily movement, gaze, gestures, and touch bind people into dyadic and group-based interactions" such that we need to "shift a level of analysis and look from individuals' expressions of emotion to the dyadic and group level" (p. 144). Arguing the benefits of DP for L2 research, Prior (2019) urges that:

> [t]aking up emotions in this way makes visible, as publicly observably and analytically available conduct, the forms they take, the communicative resources they require, the functions they serve, and the social practices they support. What emotion "is" and "means" therefore depends on how it is socially shared and grounded in situ.
>
> (p. 519)

Divisively perhaps, DP takes a strong position in considering psychology to be discernable *only* through social context; it does not interpret psychology via what is going on in people's minds but, instead, through their practices and social interactions (Wiggins, 2017). As such, DP has also been criticized as "incomplete" in its neglect of the "complex interplay among cultural, social structural, cognitive, and neurological forces" related to emotional emergence (Turner & Stets, 2005, p. 9; see also Prior, 2016).

A small-lens approach

Taking somewhat more of a middle ground, in our own field, Ushioda (2016) has recently suggested a "small lens" approach which may prove

46 *Experiential and discursive context*

equally useful in researching L2 study emotions. As one aspect of this approach, in alignment with the situatedness of DP, Ushioda (2016) argues the necessity of "a more sharply focused or contextualized angle of inquiry … in relation to particular classroom events or to evolving situated interactions" (p. 564). In aiming to afford locally based understandings of psychological phenomena in the complex social environment of particular L2 learning contexts, the small-lens approach suggests practitioner-research to offer valuable insights. As Juarrero (2002) notes, "providing a robust and detailed historical narrative of all the background and context surrounding a unique moment" intimates that "the better the explainer knows the agent, the circumstances surrounding the behavior, and how the two interacted, the more smoothly this reconstruction will proceed" (p. 226). Drawing on Tripp's (1993) outline of critical incident analysis, the small-lens approach zooms in on significant or critical episodes in learning (however, these are defined – see the next section for the ways in which I have located such events). Yet, a small-lens approach does not confine itself purely to the examination of interactions with others in social context during such significant events (as with DP) but concurrently strives for insights into the sensemaking of each unique person (Ushioda, 2020). Indeed, in outlining research in general education, Reisenzein et al. (2014) argue the need for a blending of introspective and observatory data-collection tools to illuminate from different angles the complexity of emotions, which straddle intrapsychic and social contexts. The small-lens approach, thus, endeavors to "shuttle between learner-external and learner-internal contextual processes, as our analytical lens shifts from looking globally at particular learners engaging with the surrounding environment, to homing in on particular psychological or behavioral processes within the person" (Ushioda, 2015, p. 53).

Focusing in with a small lens

The small-lens approach described in this and the following chapters builds on analysis presented in Chapter 3. Taking my cue from Imai's (2010) entreaty to look at "the *sense* that each learner interactively constructs, negotiates, and appropriates regarding an emotional experience" (p. 288 – emphasis added), the first pass over learner journals drew my attention to the writing of certain students. Through reference to specific incidents connected with the short conversations, these entries seemed to suggest emotional significance. As Finch (2010) describes, "critical events cannot be objectively identified, measured, or predicted, but are dependent on the awareness and willingness-to-observe of the observer" (p. 423). Numerous writers from our own field (e.g., Pinner & Sampson, 2020; Ushioda, 2021) have argued that classroom practitioners are uniquely placed to note such events. Although unaware of it at the time, my own selection criteria for these critical episodes were similar to those expounded by Halquist and Musanti (2010), in that each held some degree of conflict and surprised me in some way – they piqued my interest to explore further. At this stage, incidents involved such diverse experiences as feelings of resilience and growth in the face of a partner's denigration and anger, nervousness to speak giving way to enjoyment, and seemingly sudden proclamations of progress in a personality goal.

While these occurrences were intriguing by themselves, I needed to understand more about the relational context (Boiger & Mesquita, 2015; Ushioda, 2009, 2016). Hence, I examined the journal entries for all group members involved in what had been marked as significant episodes on the days in question. Through looking at the emotional qualities of the entries of all interlocutors, certain events shifted further into focus from these different perspectives. At other times, due to a lack of reference to the focal incidents, these cases were set aside. Through this process, I reduced the number of potential focal cases in consideration of the quality of data of all group members.

In addition to "homing in on particular psychological or behavioral processes within the person", the small-lens approach requires "looking globally at particular learners engaging with the surrounding environment" (Ushioda, 2015, p. 53). Building on the experiential perspectives afforded by the introspective learner journals, I had conducted video recording of small-group activity that could be used to supply dialogical and observational data. Student interaction was recorded using 360-degree video cameras placed in the middle of each group. At times, video recordings were made of only limited segments of lessons, meaning that the short conversation sessions were recorded on seven occasions across the semester. The total footage came to around 270 minutes. As Wiggins (2017) advises, rather than initially transcribing recorded data, making notes about interactions is facilitative because "the process of producing these documents can allow us to get a quick overview of our whole data set in approximately the same time as it takes to watch or listen to it in real time" (p. 93). Consequently, after each lesson, I had watched video recordings and written basic notes of student behaviors, interactions, and first impressions of what I interpreted as visible aspects of an individual's emotions and "emotional climate" in groups (Cahour, 2013).

Next, I consulted the video recordings and notes I had made about interactions connected to the significant emotional experiences of interest and more fully transcribed the conversations. Although not applying a strict DP process, I used Wiggins' (2017) three steps in transcription: (i) creating a rough orthographic, time-stamped transcript; (ii) adding more detail about the ways that things were said through an adapted form of Jefferson transcription (Jefferson, 2004 – see Appendix for transcription conventions); and (iii) adding extralinguistic and contextual details in a column to the right of utterances. A number of notes are perhaps necessary here: First, conversation analytic approaches typically stringently follow standards for transcription, such as the use of line numbers instead of times, a large quantity of notations, and no use of standard punctuation. However, as a practitioner, I wanted my representations to be accessible to other practitioners – such standards at times make transcripts look more like computer code than conversations between real people at real times. Second, while DP does not admit the inference of emotion (Prior, 2016b; Wiggins, 2017), a key aspect of my adding extralinguistic and contextual detail involved observations about the visible dimensions of emotions. In doing so, I utilized the intuitive judgment method, which makes use of people's folk-psychological competence to construe emotions from behavior and context (Reisenzein et al., 2014). Such a system of observation has been found as reliable as formal emotional coding systems, as it allows observers "to use any available cue (facial, vocal, situational context, etc.) or cue combination", which "maximally exploits the available information and best approximates the process of multicue emotion inference in everyday life" (Reisenzein et al., 2014, p. 595). This stage, thus, involved watching the video recording multiple times while transcribing, then reading and re-reading the transcription while also watching the video recording to add in additional details.

Reminding myself of the experiential context identified from the introspective data, I took notes about different parts of the transcriptions, as I worked to show "what actions were accomplished through discursive practices, how they were accomplished, and how psychological business was managed in the process of doing these actions" (Wiggins, 2017, p. 121). I endeavored to interpret the ways in which what students said and how they said it in the context of the ongoing conversation, along with their observable emotional orientations to each other, came together in the emergence of the event of interest. As I zoomed in on certain micro-events in the course of the conversation, I also connected them with particular dimensions from the journal writing of focal participants. Through this discursive process, I was able to notice the interplay of not only interlocutors' emotions but also their identities, personalities, motivations, and beliefs as they interacted over the course of the short conversation sessions. That is, I used the data to "shuttle between learner-external and learner-internal contextual processes" (Ushioda, 2016, p. 53) and build a small-lens interpretation of the emergence of the significant emotional events.

Non-linearity: shifting from anxiety to relatedness and anticipation

Experiential context

The first "particular classroom event" (Ushioda, 2016, p. 564) upon which I focus revolves around the conversation session of a male (Tsutomu) and female student (Keiko) and its connections with the overall emotional climate for these learners in the lesson concerned. Conducted early in the semester (the second lesson), the short conversation lasted a mere 2 minutes, with these students electing to discuss music artists. The two reflected on the lesson thusly:

> Tsutomu: Today, I enjoyed some activities with my partner, Keiko, because we had a common favorite Japanese artist Perfume though I was nervous at first. Therefore, I think that having common anything is good to talk with someone. In other words, this seems to make me easy in that conversation. So, if I have an opportunity next time, I will ask her what she likes more, and introduce my favorite things more and more.
>
> Keiko: Today, I worked in pairs. My partner was one of people who I had never talked with, so I felt nervous as the last class. While I and talked with him about favorite artist, we were taken a video, so I got more nervous. However, he knew songs of my favorite artist so I was very happy. I enjoyed the class with him after that. As this class, I hope that I with get along with more people. I look forward to next class.

For both of these students, it is clear that nervousness dominated their initial emotionality. While Tsutomu's reflection allows little insight into the source of this feeling, Keiko is much more explicit in noting that her partner "was one of people who I had never talked with". Despite being in the same L2 English class, Keiko and Tsutomu were in separate major cohorts at the university and, hence, had no other classes together. Keiko's writing, again, reminds me of the openness and timescales through which emotions evolve – it was not the simple presence of her partner that prompted anxiety, but the fact that even after an entire semester at the university, she still had not worked with Tsutomu. This historical context converged with an intrusive aspect of the research itself, the first use of a video camera to record groups' activities, to prompt her nervousness. On the whole, however, the emotionality of these students does not seem representative of *language* anxiety, "feelings of tension and apprehension specifically associated with second language contexts" (MacIntyre & Gardner, 1994, p. 284). This particular color of anxiety has been noted as stemming from such causes as poor pronunciation, misunderstandings in communication, or biased perceptions of proficiency (MacIntyre, 2017). Yet, the nervousness upon which these students reflect appears more generally connected to shyness in interaction with an unknown other for the first time.

Despite these feelings, a turning point in the emotional trajectories of Tsutomu and Keiko appears through the short conversation topic in which they engaged: Both note the significance of having talked about a shared interest in a certain Japanese pop music group (Perfume). Relatedness, a feeling of social affirmation through connecting with others, has been proposed as a basic psychological need (Ryan & Deci, 2002). Satisfaction of this need fosters a variety of beneficial psychological outcomes, including experiences of wellness and human flourishing (Ryan & Deci, 2017). Emergent from their short conversation, the connection fostered through a shared interest certainly appears to temper anxiety for these students. While Keiko remarks that because Tsutomu "knew songs of my favorite artist" she "was very happy", this feeling then leeches into her overall experience of the lesson: "I enjoyed the class with him after that". Tsutomu, likewise, assigns his experience of being able to "enjoy some activities with my partner" to their sharing of this interest. For both of these young people, feelings of relatedness and enjoyment then engender motivation and anticipation toward interacting with others in the future classroom. Such an interpretation would seem to align with past findings by MacIntyre and Vincze (2017), who found that pleasant emotions more often prompted motivation for L2 learners in Italy (cf. Méndez López and Peña Aguilar's 2013 situated study which also uncovered the possibilities for *unpleasant* emotions to instill motivation in specific cases).

Discursive context

Previous empirical work by Dewaele and MacIntyre (2016) has revealed that language anxiety and enjoyment "do not necessarily operate in a seesaw relationship, where one goes up and the other goes down, but rather they function somewhat independently" (p. 230). Nevertheless, there seemed to be a sharp shift from (more general) anxiety to enjoyment in this dyad's reflections, piquing my curiosity to examine the social context of their exchange (Table 4.1).

The anxiety noted by these learners in their reflections is equally evident via observation of the early stages of the short conversation, from Tsutomu's hasty first question, to a lack of eye contact between the students and looking downward (0:05–0:20). Utilizing an idiodynamic approach with stimulated recall in which student participants and their teachers viewed videos

Experiential and discursive context 51

Table 4.1 Transcript of part of Keiko and Tsutomu's short conversation

Time	Name	Speech	Context/Emotion
0:02	T:	What's = your = name?	Asks quickly, looking at K. K giggles.
0:05	K:	I'm Keiko.	Looking down at desk (embarrassed?).
0:06	T:	Keiko? (1.5) Hmm. My name is Tsutomu.	Facing K, but eyes cast down at desk.
0:14	K:	E::tto ... (Umm ...) (6.8)	K laughs (nervous?). Both looking down (at topic sheet?). Eventually K looks at T, who nods (encouragement?) – brief eye contact.
0:22	K:	I like, Perfume?	Looks to T for recognition.
0:24	T:	O::h!	Nods repeatedly, looking at K.
0:28	K:	Etto (2). Because? (3.1) They? They are *beautiful*?	Facing straight, gesturing with hands, looking for words. Turns to T at end.
0:36	T:	*Un un* (yes, yes).	Nods repeatedly, looking at K.
0:39	K:	Their music is very, *very*, ah, nice? Good?	Hits fist on open palm to stress, looking at T again.
0:46	T:	I know Perfume. I like five-seven-five, do you know?	
0:51	K:	High seven five?	Looks confused, turns to T, pair make eye contact.
0:53	T:	Five seven- Five-seven-five.	T writes it down, K looking.
0:58	K:	Ah, *Perfume*?	Tilts head to side questioning.
1:01	T:	[*Un*. I like this one, this song.]	T nods.
1:01	K:	[Ah! I *like* this, too!]	Face shows realization, points to writing.
1:05	Both:	((laughing))	Looking at each other.

of the L2 learners' presenting, Gregersen et al. (2017) found that both briefly and strongly looking downward was recognized as an indication of increasing anxiety (p. 125). Such observations are also forthcoming from the literature on emotions in general concerning anxiety and embarrassment (Keltner et al., 2019). However, after this hesitant beginning, Keiko looks to Tsutomu for first encouragement (0:14) and then for his recognition of her favorite music group, Perfume (0:22). At 0:24, Tsutomu performs a commonly recognized vocal burst – a wordless vocalization intended to express a particular emotion (Shiota & Kalat, 2018): His "O::h!" conveys his understanding and appreciation. As he nods repeatedly and faces her, Keiko becomes more animated in continuing her explanation (for instance, stressing the words "beautiful" and "very, very" and gesturing) and looks at Tsutomu for progressively longer periods (0:28–0:44). That is, through

Tsutomu's overt display of encouraging behaviors, Keiko's nervousness appears to melt away. Indeed, Dewaele and MacIntyre (2016) found pleasant feelings from encouraging and supportive peers to be a key social aspect of L2 enjoyment. Tsutomu then orients himself to Keiko's interest by attempting to convey his own favorite song by the same music group, eventually writing the title on a piece of paper. Through the video recording, it appears that Keiko is initially confused, perhaps believing that Tsutomu has instead begun to describe a different music group. When she checks – "Ah, Perfume?" (0:58) – and particularly as Tsutomu confirms and says, "this song" (1:01), she finally realizes, and the two laugh while facing each other.

In taking a more detailed look at the emergence of these students' emotions, what struck me, as a teacher, was a seeming contradiction: While the short conversation session itself lasted a mere 2 minutes, the part in which Tsutomu and Keiko discussed their shared interest was shorter still. Nevertheless, this brief period of time had an overwhelmingly important impact on their emotional trajectories for the lesson as a whole. Considered from a complexity perspective, there was *non-linearity* instead of proportional effects linearly attributable to specific, proportional causes. One possible explanation may surface through a consideration of the quality of their interaction. Drawing on Zimmerman (1998) and Richards' (2006) explorations of discoursal and social identities, Ushioda (2009) argues for the expansion of both research and pedagogy to draw out the connections between learners' L2 studies and their "transportable identities". Zimmerman (1998) defines these as "latent identities that 'tag along' with individuals as they move through their daily routines" (p. 90). These are identities held through perceived belonging to a group or being a certain type of person (such as a football fan, music lover, or someone hesitant in talking with unknown others) and which remain with us even when not overtly expressed in a particular context. In the current study, Keiko and Tsutomu's transportable identities as young, Japanese people, with a shared interest in the same music group form a key ingredient for the emergence of their pleasant emotionality. Rather than the potential associated with anxiety for "distress at their inability to be themselves and to connect authentically with other people through the limitation of the new language" (Horwitz, 2017, p. 41), these learners are able to convey important aspects of their identities as people other than language learners. In doing so, it appears that not only does their anxiety give way to relatedness and enjoyment but, moreover, to a sense of anticipation for future time they will spend in the language classroom. The seemingly trivial minute-long section of their short conversation has a disproportionately large impact on their emotional experience in the lesson on this particular day and also ripples outward to their ideas of future study.

Conclusion

The current chapter has attempted to demonstrate one way of "shifting focus" via a small lens (Ushioda, 2016). The example case suggested the non-linear development of emotions in a number of ways: Instead of linear cause-effect, a confluence of different elements came together to give rise to certain emotional trajectories, while sometimes trivial occurrences over a short timescale impacted on learners' emotions over the longer timescale of a lesson or over time in a disproportionate fashion. Additionally, combination of discursive with introspective data offered insights to the ways in which learners' emotions were not only latched to the here-and-now context of the classroom. Rather, they emerged in the moment and were understood through interactions with other aspects of their ongoing psychologies and relationships, such as a sharing of their personally important transportable identities (Zimmerman, 1998).

The next chapter builds on these beginnings by looking in detail at the ways in which learners co-construct the social and emotional context.

5 Co-adaptive emergence of emotional intersubjectivity

Despite the long-held lay notion that teachers teach, and learners learn, complexity intimates the gradual evolution of patterns without any predetermined plan or central governing agent that controls behavior (Cilliers, 1998; Larsen-Freeman & Cameron, 2008; Sampson & Pinner, 2021). What this means, in terms of L2 learning, is that while we, as teachers, might occasion various activities and exercises in which students participate, the contexts, actions, and connected emotions that emerge in the classroom self-organize across time. Emergence – the evolution of novel properties of a whole that would have been difficult to predict (de Wolf & Holvoet, 2005) – occurs on numerous levels as a representation of the dynamic, non-linear interactions making up the history of any phenomenon of interest (Larsen-Freeman & Cameron, 2008). In a reciprocal fashion, learners bring their experiences, feelings, and other psychological aspects to bear on the social context while this co-formed context additionally feeds back to impact these elements. There is a "mutually-constitutive relationship between learner and context" (Ushioda, 2011, p. 188); learners co-adapt as they change their behaviors based on their perceptions of the actions and utterances of others (Larsen-Freeman & Cameron, 2008). The (felt) noticing and adaptive actions of people in classrooms are unscripted and emergent from interaction with the (felt) social context that they form together. Such co-adaptation means that, although we may consider students as acting independently, their behavior alters the social context as a whole.

The current chapter, thus, examines in a more detailed fashion the emergence of emotions via the co-adaptive social context constructed between learners in communicative interaction. Yet, as I do so, I also aver that "instead of trying to analyze complex phenomena in terms of single or essential principles" my interpretation acknowledges "it is not possible to tell a single and exclusive story about something that is really complex" (Cilliers, 1998, p. iii).

Co-adaptive emotional intersubjectivity: enjoyment in the face of disappointment

Experiential context

This second example of taking a small-lens focus on a particular instance of emotionality revolves around two male students in the seventh lesson of the semester. Ryoto and Tomohiko had elected to discuss a conversation prompt regarding "something which disappointed you recently". Despite the unpleasant emotional valence to this topic, what caught my attention in their journals was what I interpreted as expressions of extremely pleasant emotions:

> Ryoto: I talked with a new partner. He has a high communication skills, so I talked with him pleasantly. We talked about why you are late for school. I said to him "I watched a YouTube, especially virtual YouTube, and stayed overnight". He sympathize with me. Probably, we have a good chemistry. ... I enjoyed English class so much.
>
> Tomohiko: In today's class, we changed the partner. It wasn't the first time to talk with today's partner for me. So I could do the pair work with relaxing. Today's my partner is always friendly and earnestly. Therefore we could do the pair works very smooth. He knows many English words so I thought I should study hard English. And I should emulate his attitude to English class.

Raising questions about long-term empirical fascination with the single factor of language anxiety, recent research with a broadened focus has unearthed both the variety of emotions and a predominance of pleasant over unpleasant experiences in classroom settings (Garrett & Young, 2009; MacIntyre & Vincze, 2017; Sampson, 2020). Agreeing with such findings, although the prompt for these learners dealt with "disappointment", their reflections give little sense of such an unpleasant emotion. That said, there are points of seeming tension. Both members of the dyad commence by focusing on the change of partner. Notably, Tomohiko's writing hints at his personality and the potential for anxiety in such a situation when he explicitly mentions that despite this change to new pairs, "I could do the pair work with relaxing". Boiger and Mesquita (2012) draw on a variety of past research to argue that "established relationship patterns and meanings ... may render certain appraisals more salient in a given event ... and afford particular emotional qualia" (p. 222). While this was the first time for Ryoto and Tomohiko to work together in this English class, these students had an ongoing relationship brought in from other classes at the university. Unlike Tsutomu and Keiko (Chapter 4), these students were part of the same major cohort at the university and had many of their other classes together. The introspective data suggests that this relationship formed part of the playing field for the emergence of L2 study emotions in this situation. That is, Tomohiko's feeling of relief is afforded via interactions between past experiences in the form of his developing relationship with Ryoto and the current social context. Further, the journal entries imply feelings of pleasant affect for Ryoto and Tomohiko that emerge through impressions of the other and their beliefs: Intersections between built-up understandings of their partner's personality as "always friendly and earnestly"; "has high communication skills" and beliefs of what is important for effective classroom learning to enable this dyad to "do the pair works very smooth". Congruent with my own past research (Sampson, 2019), the learners' emotional experience involved a mix of "sense-making emergent from the here-and-now as well as longer timescale processes of individualized life experiences, identities, personalities, and beliefs transported into the learning context" (p. 22).

In support of Ushioda's (2009) push to consider learners as "persons-in-context", while participating in and writing about an EFL class, the reflections of these people render the impression that their L2 identities are not foremost in their thinking. They are rounded individuals who happen to be in a (compulsory) L2 classroom. However, as Taylor's (2013) study of over 1,000 L2 English learners in Romania led her to conclude, *"unless students are allowed to be themselves ... and appreciated for what they are as real people, they are unlikely to engage genuinely in class and develop as language learners and social persons"* (p. 126 – emphasis added). In the case of the focal participants, the only overt references to *L2* identity arrive at the conclusion of their entries, yet this writing reminds me of the interplay with other identities and students "allowed to be themselves" (Taylor, 2013). It appears that Ryoto used the topic of "disappointment" to introduce an instance of tardiness due to staying up late watching YouTube. The shared understandings he felt at this juncture ("He sympathize with me") intimate the development of emotional intersubjectivities (Denzin, 1984; Imai, 2010). This process involves "an interactional appropriation of another's emotionality such that one feels one's way into the feelings and intentional feeling states of the other", joining "persons into a common, or shared, emotional field of experience" (Denzin, 1984, p. 130). This perception of a shared emotionality comes together for Ryoto as his emergent feeling toward the lesson as a whole: "Probably, we have a good chemistry. ... I enjoyed English class so much". That is, we can understand that this overall experience of a connection with his partner and pleasant affect toward the

English lesson (L2 identity) is, again, grounded in a sharing of transportable identities (Zimmerman, 1998) and the responses he perceives.

Tomohiko's entry closes with more direct reflections on language learning. He observes that Ryoto "knows many English words", suggesting that his own motivation is invigorated through such perceptions: "[S]o I thought I should study hard English. And I should emulate his attitude to English class". It is tempting to consider questions of L2 identity as front and center in such writing. Indeed, from a perspective of self, I have previously conceptualized similar ideas as representing a "revising self", proximal images of a self acting differently in the future learning context based on experiences in the present (Sampson, 2016a). However, the combination of introspective with dialogical data further illuminates the ways in which these emotions, in fact, emerged through interactions with a wider psychological context. This interplay between data sources also opens a window on emotional processes involved in the co-adapted (Larsen-Freeman & Cameron, 2008) discursive context.

Discursive context

By this point in the semester, short conversation sessions had lengthened to around 4 minutes. After some small talk, Ryoto and Tomohiko settled to discuss the topic of the conversation prompt (Table 5.1).

Complexity perspectives and a person-in-context view (Ushioda, 2009) ask us to consider phenomena relationally, to "look at the in-between" (Bodine & Kramsch, 2002, p. 91). Examining the discursive context affords such a view in a number of respects. As Mesquita (2010) emphasizes, emotions are "afforded by interactions with others or, more precisely, interactions with others as rendered meaningful by cultural meanings and practices" (p. 89). One vital way in which such cultural practices impact the conversation and resultant emotions is through the students sharing stories of disappointment related to the "small culture" of undergraduate life. Ryoto's introduction of a disappointing event at 1:14 ("I was late for university, recently, because of staying overnight") is met with expressions of sympathetic understanding from Tomohiko (1:24), shown through his elongated vocal burst "O:::h", smile, and forward lean (Goetz et al., 2010). Moreover, this aspect of the shared culture of being a university student is so relatable for Tomohiko that he describes a similar experience (2:13). In addition, recollecting Ryoto's remark in his journal, the conversation has meaning and develops its emotional value for these people through their shared understandings of another "small culture" – current popular culture. Indeed, Ryoto's introduction of the *cause* of the tardiness (watching

58 *Emotional intersubjectivity*

Table 5.1 Transcript of part of Keiko and Tsutomu's short conversation

Time	Name	Speech	Context/Emotion
1:14	R:	*Etto* (umm) (2.7) I was late for university, recently, because of staying overnight.	
1:24	T:	O:::h.	Smiling, leans forward (sympathizing?)
1:27	R:	*Etto*, I saw, I watched a YouTube, which channel is, *etto*, which channel is Hikaru.[1]	T laughs in sympathy at "YouTube", leans forward
1:36	T:	*Ya:::* Really? Hikaru?	Looks surprised (eyebrows raised)
1:40	R:	*Ichi = jikan = michatta.* (I watched it for one hour)	Looks embarrassed (awkward smile, gaze down)
1:40	T:	((laughing))	
1:42	R:	For one hour, and (1.0) virtual YouTube.	
1:46	T:	Was it interesting, about Hikaru?	Looks slightly incredulous (eyebrows raised)
1:51	R:	Hikaru? (2.3) Eh, talked with Kajisakku.	
1:56	R:	[Kajiwara.[2]]	
1:56	T:	[A::::h, I see] I see.	Looks interested (leans forward), nodding (can appreciate choice)
1:56	R:	I saw it for one hour.	Looks confident (relieved?)
2:02	T:	Ah, Kaji-	Gesturing to self (has also seen?)
2:05	R:	Because, I stay overnight.	
2:06	T:	Oh.	Nodding
2:07	R:	It's so funny for me	
2:10	T:	O::h.	Smiling
2:11	R:	to hear it.	
2:13	T:	Eh, I (1.0), I was late for classes (0.5) recently, (0.7) because (0.5) I, I stayed overnight, too.	Pointing to self, laughs when introduces same situation as R
2:28	R:	O::h.	Smiles, head forward
2:29	T:	I watched (1.2) Nogizaka Forty-Six.[3]	Looks a little embarrassed
2:34	R:	Oh, great.	Looks interested (can appreciate choice), raised slanting eyebrows
2:35	T:	So I (0.6) recently, I like read (0.5) about Nogizaka. Very recently, very recently, recently.	Looks at R hesitantly, emphasizes "recently" with gesture
2:42	R:	Recently, oh, ah.	
2:48	T:	Mmm =	
2:49	R:	What kind of song do you like in Nogizaka?	
2:52	T:	A:::h (1.4) E:::h (1.0) Because it is, er, not common, but, *poppypappappa*.	Looks relieved at question, smiles, looking into air thinking

(*Continued*)

Emotional intersubjectivity 59

Table 5.1 Continued

Time	Name	Speech	Context/Emotion
3:02	R:	Oh.	Smile
3:04	T:	((laughing)) Do you know it?	Gestures to R. Smiling
3:08	R:	Eh …	Moves head to show mystified. Smiling
3:10	T:	It is not famous.	T makes a Japanese hand gesture for "don't worry"
3:12	R:	Ah, I don't know so much.	
3:15	T:	I like Influencer?	Tilts head in a questioning fashion
3:17	R:	Ah = Influencer	Smiles in recognition. T looks relieved
3:18	T:	too.	
3:19	R:	I know a little.	
3:21	T:	Oh, really?	Raised eyebrows
3:22	T:	(2.3) Mmm. Do you, do you think =	
3:28	R:	Mm?	Tilts head to side, seems surprised
3:29	T:	Do you think, Kajisakku can, Kajisakku can, can Kajisakku =	
3:33	R:	Can reach to one million subscribers?	Nods appreciation of question
3:35	T:	Reach to … *un* (yes).	Shows a kind of realization and being impressed
3:40	R:	He wanna achieve it, he wanna achieve it so much.	
3:44	T:	*Un.* (1.1) I think he cannot =	
3:51	R:	A::h.	Seems to be thinking, deciding if agrees
3:52	T:	He can't.	Makes a waving sign with his hands signaling "no way"
3:52	R:	He reached, almost, (0.6) *eto*, (0.5) four-hundred thousand subscribers. Four-hundred thousand?	Looking up and thinking; T counting in air
4:03	T:	Oh. I don't know. I don't know? ((laughing))	
4:08			Chime sounds to mark end of conversation time
4:12	R:	Ah, but I, *demo* (but), but (0.5) I think he reach one million subscribers.	
4:18	T:	H:::e (Oh). By?	Seems surprised
4:24	R:	Because of *korabo* (collaboration) with many YouTubers and many comedians.	T nods realization

1 Hikaru is a popular Japanese YouTuber who was somewhat controversial at the time of this conversation.
2 Kajisakku is a former Japanese television comedian who became a YouTuber. His real name is Kajiwara.
3 Nogizaka46 is a Japanese female idol group consisting of, unsurprisingly, 46 members.

60 Emotional intersubjectivity

YouTube featuring Hikaru) rather than focusing on the *result* (the consequences of being late for university classes) seems to play a decisive role in edging the conversation away from overt discussion of disappointment. Tomohiko's surprised reaction (1:36) and query about the content of the YouTube (1:46) instead of focusing on the effects of being late is based in his own understandings of this small culture and also works to consolidate this conversational direction.

Another clear example of shared sociocultural understandings occurs at 3:22, as Tomohiko changes the topic by attempting to ask a question. Ryoto's interested surprise at what was indeed a sudden shift in direction is at first expressed through the murmured vocal burst "Mm?" (3:28) (Cordaro et al., 2016), with his puzzlement also conveyed by tilting his head to one side (Keltner et al., 2019). Yet, as Tomohiko tries to verbalize, Ryoto predicts and finishes the question (3:33). That is, the continuation of the conversation and consequent emotions are founded in the members' shared understandings of current YouTube culture in Japan. This incident further reminds of Tomohiko's journal reference to his impression that Ryoto "knows many English words". Tomohiko's numerous false starts – "Do you think, Kajisakku can, Kajisakku can, can Kajisakku =" (3:29) – prompt Ryoto to quickly furnish the missing verb for which it seems his partner was grasping: "Can *reach* to one million subscribers?" Tomohiko then both verbally, "Reach to ... *un* (yes)" – and physically, through facial expression – shows his realization and being impressed. Recollecting the journal data, it seems that this is one moment that has clear motivational significance for Tomohiko. Yet, rather than being some kind of pure "L2 motivation", it is through the person-in-context relationality (Ushioda, 2009), grounded in the shared understandings of YouTube culture, that this motivation emerges.

Despite the pleasant emotional tone to both the conversation in general and the participants' reflections, it is also possible to understand the hesitancy with which various transportable identities (Zimmerman, 1998) are interpolated to the conversation. Nevertheless, in congruence with Imai's (2010) study, the trepidation is mitigated as the pair regularly express emotional intersubjectivities (Denzin, 1984), altering the trajectory of both their emotions and the conversation away from explicit discussion of disappointment. It seems that they build a particular kind of intersubjectivity known as "emotional embracement" (Denzin, 1984), in which "the meanings of their sensible feelings ... are understood and even vicariously felt by each other" (p. 153). Their observable behaviors and verbalizations show appreciation of the ideas and described actions of their partner. That is, through observation of the discursive context, I was able to understand their behaviors and psychologies as co-adapting (Larsen-Freeman & Cameron, 2008), forming a supportive interactional context with each other (Ushioda, 2011a).

Emotional intersubjectivity 61

Similar patterns of emotional embracement, in the form of hesitancy giving way to relief, are evident as both Ryoto and later Tomohiko share the specific detail of their pop-culture-related transportable identities. First, when Ryoto mentions the YouTuber Hikaru, Tomohiko conveys surprise quite overtly through the Japanese vocal burst for disbelief "*Ya:::*", followed by the questioning "Really? Hikaru?" with rising intonation and a raising of his eyebrows (1:36). In fact, Ryoto's awareness that Hikaru may be a potentially problematic topic (at this historical point in time) is apparent in the previous line, when he falteringly describes, "which channel is, *etto*, which channel is Hikaru" (1:27). His initial embarrassment (witnessed through facial expressions and use of the "*-chatta*" verb form in very quick, latched Japanese) upon perceiving incredulity (1:40) gives way to relief as Tomohiko shows appreciation for YouTube involving another popular YouTuber, Kajisakku (1:51). Later in the conversation, Tomohiko also shows embarrassment as he introduces his interest in the female idol group Nogizaka46 (2:29), in particular through his hedged stressing and repeating of the word "recently" (2:35). This hesitancy changes to relief when it seems he understands Ryoto's sanctioning of the topic by his asking a question (2:49) and then again as Ryoto expresses recognition of one of the songs of the idol group (3:17).

As I concurred at the beginning of this chapter with the writing of Cilliers (1998), "it is not possible to tell a single and exclusive story about something that is really complex" (p. iii). A final, nuanced perspective on these learners' interactions might, thus, also be offered by considering empirical work related to the particular culture of Japanese conversational style. Machi's (2012, 2019, 2020) research into the informal conversations of Japanese speakers who are close friends brings to light certain patterns: Such interlocutors show a tendency to connect each other's utterances via repetition and co-construction, especially when involved in discussion of a familiar topic. Both processes are evident in Tomohiko and Ryoto's interactions, such as Tomohiko's repetition of "Hikaru?" to denote surprise and confirm (1:36); Ryoto's similar duplication of "Hikaru?" to confirm (1:51); and Ryoto's repeating of the song title "Ah = Influencer" to emphasize recognition (3:17). Equally, it might be surmised that after Tomohiko shows a great deal of hesitation in describing that he has only recently started watching YouTube involving the female idol group Nogizaka (2:35), Ryoto's repetition of the word "recently" shows his acceptance and a form of sympathy for his partner's embarrassment. As previously touched upon, another instance of connecting utterances occurs when Ryoto finishes Tomohiko's question (3:29), co-constructing to continue the conversation. Machi (2020) argues that such processes in Japanese conversation give rise to "the creation of sympathy and rapport" as "the speakers' utterances and ideas are connected and shared to the degree that they see the situation from the same point of view" (pp. 18–19). It is highly possible that Ryoto and Tomohiko carry over such tendencies from their native language to their English short conversation, fostering the kind of "good chemistry" or intersubjectivity to which Ryoto refers in his reflection.

In their fluid, relational emergence, the emotional intersubjectivities evident remind of Bodine and Kramsch's (2002, p. 91) reference to the W. B. Yeats poem "Among School Children", in which we are challenged: How can we tell the dancer from the dance? The analysis suggests that the emotions of these two students both support and are supported by the discursive context in constant interaction with aspects of their ongoing identities.

Conclusion

Much L2 learning is by its very nature dependent on interactions between members forming a communicative dyad or group. The current chapter furnishes a situated glimpse of the radically socially impacted nature of L2 study emotions through such interactions. Analysis of discursive data shone a light on the ways in which students' (emotional) moves during the short conversation session were both afforded by and acted on those of the other through their social interactions as they co-adapted (Larsen-Freeman & Cameron, 2008) and, thus, co-formed the social context (Ushioda, 2011a, 2015). One way in which this process was evident was in the observation of emotional intersubjectivities (Denzin, 1984) developing and displayed across the course of the conversation. The analysis reinforces my argument throughout this book that if we are to do justice to researching L2 study emotions, we must investigate the ways they emerge within the social context of learning.

The following chapter focuses the small lens one turn further, adding depth through a look at the proximal historical context to the emergence of a significant emotional event.

6 Widening the lens
The (re)construction of anxiety and enjoyment

As introduced and then illustrated in the previous two chapters, a small-lens approach to research provokes us to investigate specific classroom events of interest in a more complex, dynamic fashion. We work to gain a detailed vision of the social contextual interactions through which emotions emerge. In addition to the present, discursive social context, we also need to contemplate the relationships in which interactional events (and corresponding emotions) are embedded (Boiger & Mesquita, 2015; Mesquita & Boiger, 2014). Moreover, the small-lens approach urges us to mesh these social insights with a picture of the internal psychological processes of individuals involved in the phenomenon of interest.

Yet, MacIntyre et al. (2021) advise that from a complexity perspective, researchers are required to "consider how a process unfolds over a chosen period of time" (p. 17); we need to "examine the dynamics in action and the actual processes of change" (p. 23). It is insufficient to explore a phenomenon involving psychological and social beings out of its temporal context. It is the embodiment of its history, wherein a learner's "past is co-responsible for their present behavior" (Cilliers, 1998, p. 4). In congruence with complexity thinking, Ushioda (2015, 2016) has also stressed the importance of bearing in mind that significant or critical events occur in the wider context of the ongoing *history* of interactions. As she reminds, "while the critical incident constitutes the immediate context of analysis, the analysis itself is likely to have wider contextual perspectives, extending back to the shared history of interactions among the persons involved" (Ushioda, 2016, p. 572). The time window concerned in such a history of interactions may be anything from mere seconds in length (as in the discursive context). However, our emotions emerge over longer periods also, not purely as an instantaneous occurrence in reaction to some external trigger in the present. They are grounded in our past experiences, relationships, and continuing psychology, including projections into the future (Baumgartner et al., 2008; Sampson, 2019b), as we shall see in the current chapter.

Narrating anxiety into enjoyment

As a result of their research in the Japanese tertiary EFL context, King and Smith (2017) have argued the value of non-public (pair or small-group) opportunities for meaningful communication. They contend that such opportunities might promote acceptance and decrease the potential for social anxiety and silence (pp. 104–105). In offering learners the chance for interactions via which they might express their identities and co-construct their own, authentic content (Pinner, 2016a), the short conversation segment of my lessons seemed to align well. Moving to the eleventh lesson of the semester, then, the reflections of one student connected with his experiences during the short conversation session, thus, captured my interest. Akito (a male) was working in a three-member group with two other male students, Takuya and Keigo. What was perplexing in the writing of this focal-learner was what seemed to be a significant episode of anxiety. In my role as a teacher, and particularly in light of the comparatively few mentions of anxiety related to the short conversation segment of lessons, my curiosity was naturally piqued. I wanted to uncover more about the emergence of this experience in the hope of better supporting learners in my future classrooms. Yet, as I shifted the small lens (Ushioda, 2016) iteratively between the experiential and discursive data, it offered a vital, more nuanced perspective on the construction of Akito's emotions.

Experiential context

As the following extract shows, Akito devoted his entire written reflection to thinking back on his emotional experiences in the short conversation session:

> Akito: Even in this group, I still got anxious when I talk about my favorite. I should have confidence in my loving them. I want to use English to communicate with people who is interested in subculture that is different with mine in the future. And, I noticed that I can talk more in other classroom activities like textbook than in Short Conversation. It means that I am good at official speaking compared with chat. It is right in my speaking Japanese, too. Therefore, to sum up, I should know some slangs, and I will talk with others more smoothly. But, I was glad you give us a lot of time to talk with other members some information in short conversation. I could tell information in my group and in this lesson enjoyably.

It appears that Akito was "anxious when I talk about my favorite" during the short conversation, engendering disappointment and perhaps a kind of shame in himself that he "should have confidence in my loving them". While past research may nudge us to jump to the conclusion that this is possibly a case of additional language anxiety (Horwitz et al., 1986), the writing of the other group members provides the foundation for a different explanation. As a matter of fact, this group had chosen the same topic for conversation as the students upon which I focused in Chapter 4: favorite musicians. In the present case, the reflection of one of the other members of this group, Keigo, suggests that a reason for Akito's hesitation may have been more connected with his choice of a less-recently-popular artist. As Keigo noted, "My teammates like a little old singer". Indeed, the other group member, Takuya, similarly mentioned that he "was worried about if I get my group members' sympathy or not because my favorite musician retired from the music world about 40 years ago". Nevertheless, it is amidst these feelings of anxiety and disappointment that Akito ponders his motivation to use English in the future to be able to "communicate with people who is interested in subculture that is different with mine". He then, moreover, provides a crucial metanarrative of his sensemaking connected with his experience of anxiety. In the focal episode, he notices that he is subjectively more proficient at "official speaking", meaning that he "can talk more in other classroom activities like textbook than in Short Conversation". Akito's own words distinctly reject the possibility of *additional* language anxiety: "It is right in my Japanese speaking, too". His reflection gives the sense that elements of his personality in general impacted his ability to speak fluently during the short conversation session (as compared with other segments in the lesson) rather than any L2-specific aspect. Thus, this appears reminiscent of what is known in personality psychology as a "characteristic adaptation", "motivational, social-cognitive, and developmental constructs that are more specific than dispositional traits and that are contextualized in time, place, and/or social role" (McAdams, 2010, p. 177). Akito gives voice to a realization that he is perhaps more generally able to verbalize in structured situations (such as when discussing textbook exercises) compared with freer conversation, regardless of whether this is in his first or additional language. This seems an important realization, and he displays his motivation to try to alter this aspect of his personality by "know[ing] some slangs" in order to help him "talk with others more smoothly".

What further caught my attention in Akito's reflection is that he both starts and finishes with a focus on the group. In particular, in his very first sentence he mentions that "*Even in this group,* I *still* got anxious" (emphasis added). This sentence seemed to imply the importance of time – there was something about *this* group that made it surprising for Akito to, nevertheless, feel worried. This group had been together for three lessons. As I examined Akito's previous reflections, I unearthed something vital to understanding his emotions on the day in question: Prior to joining his current group, he had a very unpleasant experience with a different student. In the sixth lesson, Akito noted that "my new group member is aggressive person". The nature of this "aggressiveness" is then revealed in his reflection on experiences during the short conversation in Lesson 7:

> I found new, personal problem today. In the short conversation time, I could not answered how I spent free time. I was sometimes pointed it up by my group partner. He said my speed of communication was so slow. He was angry. Then, I should have told false thing ... I will improve this from next lesson.

While in the Lesson 6 reference he had described this partner as "aggressive", in Lesson 7, Akito seems to assign all the blame to himself, and his disappointment is stark. However, when he moved to the new focal group, he appeared to begin to realize the importance of the others in co-forming possibilities for communicative interactions and emotional experience: "Today, new group member was cheerful and cackle, so I could face this lesson comfortably. On Short Conversation, I could talk with them smoothly" (Lesson 9). Again, moving to the focal session, Akito concluded that "I could tell information in my group and in this lesson enjoyably". Thus, I wanted to explore the discursive context for this reflection.

Discursive context (and moving back to the experiential)

During the short conversation session, Akito was sitting in the center of the three-student group, with Takuya on the left and Keigo on the right. The members had chosen the topic of favorite musicians before the session commenced. Although Takuya and Keigo also presented ideas about their own preferences at other points in the conversation, the following excerpt focuses primarily on Akito's speaking turn (Table 6.1).

Extending over a relatively protracted period (just over 2 minutes), Akito's contributions to the short conversation display a variety of the hallmarks of increasing anxiety. At the commencement of his turn, both Takuya and Keigo look pointedly at Akito in the center of their group (0:00). Akito appears, to some extent, to try not to notice but glances quickly left and right and then gestures inquiringly to himself. Keigo nods affirmation, prompting a period of silence during which Akito shows signs of increasing anxiety as he thinks – by turn crossing his arms, stroking his chin, and looking up at the ceiling (Gregersen et al., 2017). While Keigo maintains his gaze on Akito and leans toward him in an apparent show of anticipation

Table 6.1 Transcript of Akito's main speaking turn during short conversation

Time	Name	Speech	Context / Emotion
0:00	A:	(1.5)	T&K both looking at A. A looks rapidly left and right, notices. Gestures to self with hand
0:02	K:	(4.0)	Nods
0:07	A:	H:::mm, h:::mm. (8.0)	A arms crossed. Raises eyes to ceiling repeatedly, strokes chin. K scratches head, continues looking at A (turned toward). T looks from A down to desk, and back again
0:17	K:	So ...	Waves hand around (encouraging?)
0:19	A:	My (1.4), my (3.8)	Drops hand from chin, crosses arms
0:26	A:	Recent, recently, erm, my (gulps) favorite, err (1.0),	A pushes glasses up, closes and reopens eyes. Keeps one hand gesturing in front of body as commences speaking, then crosses arms. Both K&T turned toward A.
0:34	A:	artist is (0.8) *nandarouna*? (I wonder?) (5.0)	A raises hand to chin
0:44	A:	*Ma* (well) (3.0)	Waves hand around in front of face. Face looks worried yet resolved
0:48	A:	Makihara Noriyuki.[1]	Makes eye contact with K. Smiles slightly as says
0:50	K: T:	[Oh yeah] [A::::h]	T&K smile, nod recognition
0:51	A:		Looks relieved, smiles, waves hand in front of body
0:54	A:	Ah (0.6) my (0.8) parents (1.0), parents, parents? parents dig it.	A waving hand in front of body. Looks up at ceiling then down at desk as repeating "parents"
1:04	K:	Ah ah ah. (2.5)	Nodding
1:07	A:	The (0.6) °*nani hanashitara ii?*° (What should I say?)	Raises hand to chin. T&K both turned toward, looking at face
1:11	A:	(5.0)	Face raised, looks at hand, then waves hand around in front of face as looking down (thinking?). T&K still looking at face
1:17		(9.0)	T&K look down at desk
1:27	A:	°*Doushiyou?*° (What should I do?) (3.0)	Looks up, raises hand to chin. T&K quickly raise gaze to look at A's face
1:31	K:	What's the best music?	
1:32	A:	(5.0)	Stroking chin, looking up (thinking?)
1:38	K:	What music do you like best?	
1:41	T:	Yeah, of Maki?	Looking at A

(*Continued*)

Table 6.1 Continued

Time	Name	Speech	Context / Emotion
1:43	A:	I like (5.0), Mmm (1) I think I like (7.0), from his music I like song-	A hand stroking chin, looking up (thinking?). T&K looking at A
1:57	A:	°*Onaji topikku?*° (Same topic?)	Looks at K
1:59	K:	A-huh.	Nods slightly. T folds arms
2:03	A:	*Boku ga Ichiban Hoshikatta Mono.*	Waves hand in front of face (I've got it!). T&K both look at A's face. Smiling as says
2:07	T:	[A:::h a:::h]	Nods recognition
	K:	[A:::h yeah]	Nods recognition
2:09	A:	[I like] this song.	
	K:	[I like-]	
2:10	K:	Yeah, I like it, too.	
2:13	A:	How about you?	Looks at K

1 Makihara Noriyuki ("Maki") is a Japanese pop singer-songwriter active since the 1990s.

(Keltner & Shiota, 2003), Takuya seems somewhat embarrassed by the silence, switching from looking at Akito to down at the desk (Keltner et al., 2019). Eventually (0:17), as Keigo appears about to offer some verbal support (beginning with "So" and gesturing with his hand), Akito starts speaking. Nevertheless, he continues to display previously recognized signs of nervousness, as he repeats words (0:26 – "recently"; 0:54 – "parents"), frequently intersperses utterances with pauses, and includes Japanese (0:34 – "*nandarouna*"; 0:44 – "*Ma*")(Gregersen et al., 2017). In fact, the start of this turn is punctuated by a quite obvious gulp (0:26). The moment before Akito eventually introduces his favorite musical artist witnesses a facial expression showing his resolve, as he purses his lips and lowers his eyebrows (Keltner et al., 2019). As he pronounces "Makihara Noriyuki" (0:48), Akito smiles slightly, one of the few times during his turn. Takuya and Keigo's verbalizations at 0:50 ("A:::h"; "Oh yeah"), combined with facial expressions (opening eyes and mouth wide) and nodding send a clear signal of their appreciation of this choice (Goetz et al., 2010; Shiota & Kalat, 2018). Once again, this appreciation intimates the instantiation of shared knowledge about this artist active since before these students were born, as the members' transportable identities (Zimmerman, 1998) as Japanese people of the same generation are engaged. The recognition, in turn, elicits an expression of relief from Akito, prompting him to further continue by explaining why he is fond of this particular singer. That is, amidst Akito's apparent anxiety, his group members' displays of support seem to encourage him to maintain communication.

However, despite the potential for this moment to act as a turning point in the short conversation, at 1:07 another long silence ensues. It seems as if Akito did in fact have something planned to say, as he starts with, "The", though it is unclear why he discontinues his utterance. It might be surmised that his anxiety returns, as past research has found the negative effects of anxiety on the retrieval of information in language production situations (see MacIntyre, 2017). During this lengthy pause, besides Akito occasionally breaking the silence with rhetorical questions in Japanese, there is nevertheless a great deal going on in terms of bodily actions seeming to display the emotionality of the group members. Akito waves his hand around in front of his face, apparently thinking, and also shifts his gaze downward, intimating increasing nervousness (Gregersen et al., 2017). As a progressively lengthy amount of time passes, the other group members also eventually shift their gaze down from Akito's face to the desk. At 1:27, Akito rhetorically poses the question "*Doushiyou*?" (What should I do?), while raising his eyes to the ceiling and stroking his chin. It seems that this display of embarrassed confusion nudges Takuya and Keigo to support him, as they return their gaze to Akito, with Keigo posing the question, "What's the best music?" (1:31). In response, Akito again shows that he is thinking by stroking his chin and looking up (Ehrlichman & Micic, 2012). Notwithstanding, as time again passes, it seems Keigo may have determined that the question was not understood, leading him to paraphrase (1:38) and Takuya to add the "Yeah, of Maki?" (1:41). Although Akito then starts to answer the question (1:43), at the last moment, it appears that he has indeed been unsure as to whether he should be introducing a song by Makihara Noriyuki (the same topic) or what he thinks is the "best music" (a potentially different topic involving a different artist). While presenting his confusion by quickly tilting his head to one side (Keltner et al., 2019; Rozin & Cohen, 2003), Akito checks by asking in Japanese, "*Onaji topikku*?" (Same topic?), with Keigo confirming, "A-huh". Akito then waves his arm in front of his face in a gesture representing "I've got it!", and smiles as he conveys his favorite song. While Keigo and Takuya both nod and verbalize their recognition with the common Japanese affirmation "A:::h!", Keigo finally additionally emphasizes that "Yeah, I like it, too" (2:10).

All in all, as a teacher watching the video of these students' conversation, I must admit that it made me a little uneasy. Although Akito had referred in his reflection to the enjoyment he felt with this group during the short conversation session, his silences and inability to start a speaking turn in fact seemed highly representative of language anxiety (Gregersen et al., 2017; Horwitz et al., 1986). Nevertheless, in combination with the experiential data, I was able to understand that it is vital to gain insights into how the people involved in such an episode themselves make sense of it and construct emotional meaning dynamically (Denzin, 1984). Akito's subjective experience of enjoyment is relative and contextualized in time: In comparison with his previous experiences with a more "aggressive" interlocutor, he felt comfortable in this group. As noted earlier, the social dimension of L2 study enjoyment is underpinned by feeling that peers are supportive and encouraging (Dewaele & MacIntyre, 2016). Indeed, Akito's reflection that "I could tell information in my group and in this lesson enjoyably", and interpretations of the discursive data align with research from general psychology into self-disclosure in young adults. Vijayakumar and Pfeifer (2020) summarize that "feedback from others not only helps them validate the appropriateness of their feelings, thoughts and behaviors, but also supports the development of close relationships" (p. 136). While from an outsider point of view on the group, the support may seem rather threadbare and subtle at times, what is important is how Akito himself perceives it and the enjoyment that he feels. Dewaele and MacIntyre's (2016) research similarly draws attention to such subjective interpretations, as they found that "enjoyment for one might not be enjoyment for all" (p. 227). Akito's perceptions and emotionality are vitally located amidst his other experiences (such as those with his previous partner). As Simsek and Dörnyei (2017) argue, a "bird's-eye-view" of language learning experiences can play a crucial "redemptive" function in "turn[ing] any negative trajectories into more positive ones" (p. 66). The activity of writing reflections each lesson may have encouraged Akito to form a new, more pleasant metanarrative on his experiences and the role of the group.

Conclusion

From a complexity perspective, Juarrero (2002) argues that:

> Yesterday's choices affect today's options, but choices made today will also bias those options available tomorrow. The environment coevolves with us ... In a process of continuous landscape reconfiguration, each step enhances or diminishes the downstream options available to the organism. That is, each choice alters both the availability and probability of future steps. We are not passive products of either the environment or external forces. In a very real sense we contribute to the circumstances that will constrain us later on.
>
> (pp. 252–253)

In considering such circumstances, the current chapter has expanded Ushioda's (2016) small-lens approach to include aspects of the experiential, discursive, and historical context in interpreting the emergence of an instance of significant emotionality for an individual learner. While I focused in quite some detail on this one student, experiential data from other learners and discursive data from the group also illuminated different perspectives and social aspects of this critical episode. The historical approach implies that, reminiscent of Denzin's (1984) arguments, "emotion is located in the personal biography" of individuals in social context, wherein "contextualizing isolates its meaning for them, presenting it in terms of their languages, meanings, and understandings" (p. 10).

Chapter 7 continues this more historical perspective by developing the intersections between L2 study emotions and an agentic angle on personality.

7 Widening the lens
L2 study emotions and agentic personality

The intersections between L2 learning and personality have been sporadically investigated over the years. Despite an intuitive sense that personality will have an impact on students' actions and language development, findings have been inconclusive at best and, at times, even contradictory (see e.g., Dewaele, 2013 and Dörnyei & Ryan, 2015 for overviews). What, then, of the connections between personality and L2 study emotions? And if, as Larsen-Freeman (2019) emphasizes from a complexity perspective, "agency is always related to the affordances in the context, and thus inseparable from them" (p. 65), how might the context play a role in the evolution of personality (and, thus, emotions) over time? While centered on a critical emotional episode, in the current chapter I thus widen the lens further to extend the historical focus to the entire semester. My interpretations allow me to develop a more agentic view of the interactions between ongoing, revising understandings of personality and emotions connected with L2 study.

Immediate experiential context

In what follows, I center on the situated emergence of an emotionally significant episode for one male learner, Kazuma. On the day in question (Lesson 11), he was grouped together with another male (Makito) and a female student (Wakana). Kazuma's reflection on his experiences reveals a pleasant emotional tone in a number of different areas:

> Today's lesson, I tried to act positively. In conversation time and other activity time, I tried to speak first. In conversation time, we spoke about movies. We all like Ghibli movies and music. The girl in our group mixed The Cat Returns and Kiki's Delivery Service in her brain. It was so funny. She said *Neko-no-Takkyuubinn*. But recently we don't have enough time to watch a movie. So, we could talk about it only a little. But still, I seem that I become to act positively in lesson!

DOI: 10.4324/9781003306955-7

Emotions and agentic personality 73

Relatedness through transportable identities

As with cases in the previous chapters, the majority of Kazuma's journal entry for this lesson revolves around his experiences during the short conversation session. Firstly, there are moments of enjoyment evident, as he alludes to an incident when one of his group members, Wakana, muddled the names of two films. This episode is also connected to feelings of relatedness (Ryan & Deci, 2002) and the instantiated transportable identities (Zimmerman, 1998) of these learners as young Japanese people with an interest in the movies of a famous Japanese animation company (Studio Ghibli): Kazuma's reference is inclusive as he writes, "*We all like* Ghibli movies and music" (emphasis added). Wakana's journal revealed that she concurred with this sense of shared appreciation, stating "*We* like Ziburi movies" (emphasis added). Feelings of disappointment, tempered with a sense of affiliation, can also be inferred concerning another dimension of the transportable identities of these learners. Kazuma is inclusive as he bemoans not being able to watch movies – "recently *we* don't have enough time to watch a movie" (emphasis added) – and describes the impact this had on the conversation. His sense of relatedness is echoed in Makito's journal entry for the day, which also provides a hint of one of the qualities of this feeling, as undergraduates with little time to watch movies because of many assignments: "We talk about recent watching movie, *all of us* couldn't watch, because *we* are busy. *We all* have many, many reports!" The reflections of Kazuma and his group members hint at the shared understandings of these people as university students in general (rather than purely L2 learners) in a particular historical context – at this point in time, as the end of the second semester of their first year at university was drawing to a close, they found themselves flooded with assignments for many of their classes. That is, their emotions of disappointment tinged with affiliation and concurrent actions inside an L2 class cannot be understood divorced from the wider educational and temporal setting (van Lier, 2004).

A sense of progress

Despite the detail with which Kazuma recollected these specific parts of the lesson, it was another, more general aspect to his entry that most caught my attention. Bordering either side of his writing concerning the short conversation, he stresses his motivation to put in effort across the lesson as a whole. His entry begins: "Today's lesson, I tried to act positively. In conversation time and other activity time, I tried to speak first". In addition, although he seems disappointed that he and his group members were not able to talk in more detail about movies, he finishes his entry by reflecting excitedly, "But still, I seem that I become to act positively in lesson!"

A little context is necessary to understand the momentousness: As part of the broader action research, at the start of the semester, students had brainstormed hopes for "ideal classmates" (Murphey et al., 2014). These hopes were actions they wanted their peers to take in order to make a classroom environment more conducive to communicative language learning. These had been collated, and students were then shown and encouraged to individually choose a behavioral ideal upon which to act in each lesson. In truth, in spite of past findings of various motivational and emotional benefits through introducing such an activity (Murphey et al., 2014; Murphey & Iswanti, 2014; Peragine, 2019; Sampson, 2018), the data from this class suggested few students took it up with vigor. Nevertheless, even a preliminary scan of Kazuma's prior journal entries hinted that he contrasted in several respects: First, he had selected an ideal for almost every lesson of the semester up to this point. More intriguingly, while other students chose a variety of ideals, Kazuma always chose the same hope for action – to "act positively". Finally, despite such dedication, he had only ever written about a sense of achievement of his ideal once. My own past research in this area has found that learners frequently focus on the ideal classmates hopes as behavioral goals to achieve each lesson and, hence, reflect on the degree of accomplishment (Sampson, 2018). Yet, Kazuma had only intimated such a sense of achievement at the very start of the semester. Hence, his excited proclamation at the conclusion of this entry that he had a feeling of progress seemed notable.

Rather than being a fleeting experience situated in the moment, Kazuma's phrasing – "but still", "become to act" – intimates the historical context to be crucial to understanding the emergence of this emotion. Therefore, I next examined the nearest immediate temporal setting for this intense feeling – the video recording available for Lesson 11 as well as data for the other lessons (Lessons 9 and 10) that these members were together as a group.

Proximal historical context: discursive context and experiences over a lesson series

In Lesson 11, Kazuma was sitting on the left of his three-student group, with Makito in the center and Wakana on the right. The video recording on this day was limited to the short conversation session, for which the group had already chosen a topic (movies recently watched). The transcription begins with an announcement from myself as teacher (Table 7.1).

Emotions and agentic personality 75

Table 7.1 Transcript of part of Kazuma, Makito and Wakana's short conversation

Time	Name	Speech	Context / Emotion
0:00	Tch:	Let's do these conversations for five minutes. Remember, last week, <u>lots</u> of Japanese, so <u>this week</u>, more English, <u>ok</u>? This is your <u>last</u> English listening lesson for this year, so let's finish by using <u>lots of English</u>. Ok? Five minutes …	K is looking down at his book on his desk
0:26	M:	Ok, what movie did you go see?	M turns to K and asks. Throughout exchange, W turns toward them, but does not interact verbally
0:31	K:	I didn't see a movie, but I want to see, ah, watch a movie, four days … (3) future.	M smiles slightly when he realizes K has not watched movie recently. K waves arms to imply passing of time
0:43	M:	After?	
0:45	K:	After, yeah, after. I want to watch, Hiroaka?	Smiles (Embarrassed?). Checking intonation
0:48	M:	Oh, yeah.	
0:49	K:	Watch that movie, so. I couldn't watch, ahh (1.5) watch, ahh before, I couldn't see, so (1.2) now, nowadays, this time, I want to watch … (3.5) *zettai*.	Continual "thinking" gesture with hands. Looks questioningly at M when using Japanese
1:19	M:	Absolutely.	
1:20	K:	Absolutely, yeah.	Looks a little disappointed (eyes down)
1:23	K:	What have you watched a movie?	
1:26	M:	Recently, I didn't watch movie anything. So, <u>now,</u> I don't see a drama also, yeah, I don't watch drama and movies. <u>Recently,</u> I don't watch, ah, anything else on TV or movie show. How about you?	Laughs when also has not watched movie. Sitting back, head up. W nods agreement At end, turns to W
1:46	W:	*Nanmo nai* (Nothing). I didn't watch some.	Sitting back. K and M smile in sympathy
1:49	M:	Yeah.	
1:51	W:	I don't have time, (1.3) my time, so I can't go (2.5) so far.	Sitting back, turns to center of group
1:58	K:	Anywhere.	
2:00	W	I can't see any movie.	Looks down (disappointed?). K eyes track quickly upward – thinking?
2:05	K:	Do you have favorite movie?	

(*Continued*)

76 *Emotions and agentic personality*

Table 7.1 Continued

Time	Name	Speech	Context / Emotion
2:08	M:	Favorite movie? Ah (1.2), favorite movie (1), movie-	W seems to be thinking, looking at ceiling
2:15	K:	I like [Ghibli]	Leans back
2:16	W:	[Ghibli]	Both say at same time. K smiles
2:17	K:	Ghibli. I like Ghibli, too. *Momonoke Hime* (Princess Momonoke) is ...	Leans forward and to the side (toward center of group)
2:20	M:	Oh yeah. Oh, yeah. [Me too]	Everyone smiling (cannot see W), nodding, animated, leaning forward
2:22	W:	[Me too]	Leaning forward
2:23	M:	I love *Mononoke Hime*. (2.3)	After short flurry, a little pause
2:27	W:	Ah, um (3) *Nekono Takyuubin* (cat delivery-service).	Leans forward. Pointing at herself and thinking
2:29	K/M:	O:::h! (2.1)	Nodding agreement, appreciation
2:32	M:	Eh, *Nekono Takyuubin*?	Looks inquiringly at W (head tilted)
2:35	W:	Ah! *Majo no Takyuubin*!	Laughing as realizing, everyone laughing
2:38	M:	*Nekono Ongaeshi*? Didn't you confused?	Everyone laughing
2:40	W:	Yes, I like both! I like both!	Laughing, K laughing
2:45	M:	Yeah, yeah, I love it.	Head up
2:47	K:	Ghibli's movies, ah, good song.	
2:51	M/W:	Yeah, yeah, yeah.	Everyone nodding agreement
2:55	K:	I like it. So, yeah, my favorite musician is Ghibli's music. I like Ghibli's music, yeah.	Everyone nodding

Expressions of relatedness

Although bound to only part of the short conversation session, the transcript further illuminates various dimensions of the development of the emotionality in this group on the day in question. Recollecting the enjoyment and amusement about which Kazuma reflected in his journal entry, the injection to the conversation of the topic of Studio Ghibli witnesses two rapid exchanges (2:25–2:24; 2:29–2:41). In combination with facial expressions such as Duchenne smiling (smiling with one's eyes as well as mouth), laughter, and bodies leaned forward, these brief explosions of interaction seem to be representative of pleasant emotionality such as interest and excitement (Keltner et al., 2019; Reeve, 1993). In addition, the relatedness felt through a sharing of similar transportable identities is clear throughout as all students nod in agreement and especially at 2:16, as Kazuma and Wakana proclaim "Ghibli" at exactly the same moment. Makito, who had up to that point been struggling to arrive at an idea for his favorite movie (2:08–2:14), concurs when Kazuma offers the example of *Mononoke Hime* (2:20), with Wakana agreeing also (2:22). This entire exchange, and the pleasant emotionality emergent, moreover, during the "muddling" (2:27–2:40) is rooted in the transportable identities of these people as young Japanese for whom the movies of this particular studio form a ubiquitous experience from childhood (Rendell & Denison, 2018).

The other aspect of affiliation via transportable identities about which all members had reflected in their journals – as undergraduate students with too much on their plates – is also apparent in numerous exchanges: As Kazuma commences with "I didn't see a movie", to which Makito smiles knowingly (0:31); Makito's lengthy exposition of not having time to watch any movies or television programs (1:26), in which he stresses the words "now" and "recently", and during which Wakana nods appreciatively; and Kazuma and Makito's sympathetic smiles when, finally, Wakana also divulges that she has not been able to watch anything ("Nanmo nai" – 1:46). The disappointment hinted at in their journal entries seems almost more bemusement as they are interacting – despite having established the topic for their conversation as movies recently watched, none of them is actually able to directly address it. This interpretation would seem to match with past research, which has found a tendency for Japanese people to qualify their display of unpleasant emotions through slight smiles and laughter (Matsumoto et al., 2005, 2008).

Proactivity

As I have argued previously, complexity perspectives prompt our cognizance of the dynamic interconnectedness of a vast array of elements in the context of the emergence of any phenomenon at the point in time at which we observe it (Larsen-Freeman & Cameron, 2008; Morin, 2008). Focusing the small lens to home in on the event of significant emotionality, situated throughout these other episodes is evidence of Kazuma's proactivity. Right from the beginning of the conversation, in response to Makito's inquiry, Kazuma admits that he has not watched any movies recently. What is of note, here, is that he then immediately continues by adapting the direction of the conversation to his future plans (0:31). That is, it seems that Kazuma had been forward-thinking in analyzing the agreed topic in the short time before the conversation began and was prepared to expand on a related tangent. Additionally, while he returns to the original focus when asking Makito (1:23), it became increasingly clear this topic was not going to generate much detail from the group members. At 2:00, as Wakana is also disappointed at not having watched a movie, Kazuma's eyes track rapidly diagonally upward, seeming to suggest quickly thinking (Ehrlichman & Micic, 2012). Perhaps as a result of this thinking, he prompts a change in direction to "favorite movies" (2:05). Although the other interlocutors seemed to be struggling in response, Kazuma then offers his own example of favorite movies (2:15). Both of these actions draw Wakana into the conversation (and lead to the humorous mix up in movie titles) – in contrast to her physical expressions during her own relating of not having watched anything recently (sitting back, looking down), in these exchanges she leans forward and seems intent (Keltner et al., 2019). Finally, in spite of it turning out to be a dead end for the conversation, Kazuma is also the only student to add a reason for liking the movies of this animation studio (2:47). In sum, the pleasant emotionality that all three group members implied experiencing connected with the discussion of Studio Ghibli emerges through their interactions yet is heavily afforded by Kazuma's efforts to "act positively" in this lesson.

Teacher interjection

As I engaged with the data, I was also reminded of ideas of heterochrony, wherein long timescale processes might play a role in a triggering effect during a much shorter-timescale activity (Lemke, 2000). An incident not mentioned by Kazuma in his reflection for Lesson 11, though apparent from the dialogical data, involved my own initial exhortation as teacher for students to use English (0:00–026). I began by imploring, "Remember, last week …?" Examination of my journal entry for the previous lesson unearthed a feeling that there had been little use of English in a number of groups at various times. Hence, near the end of that lesson, I had been motivated to engage in "a bit of a talk with the whole class about how they didn't need to practice their Japanese" (TJ, Lesson 10). As most teachers would no doubt agree, such interventions at critical points aimed at raising behavioral issues with class members have the potential to go either way in terms of fostering actions more conducive to the learning teachers intend. As a matter of fact, as I had continued, "Makito, in particular, was talking animatedly about music groups in entirely Japanese. Even after I stopped the class, he persisted". In contrast, perhaps influenced by the excess of L1-use in his group context, in response, Kazuma had reflected: "Exactly, I also sometimes spoke in Japanese when I troubled in telling what I wanted to talk about. But then, it has no meaning. I knew. So, I will make an effort to continue speaking English more than before" (LJ, Lesson 10). Kazuma's perseverance with trying to "act positively" did not necessarily imply using

Emotions and agentic personality 79

the L2. However, my encouragement before the short conversation session in Lesson 11 may have reminded him of his intentions to use more English from the previous week. In parallel with my previous experiences (Sampson, 2016a, b), it seems that my interjection resonated as a kind of "tipping point" (Gladwell, 2000) for some students, not least Kazuma. This sequence of events and sensemaking, in turn, formed part of the psychological context for his actions and emergent emotions on the day in question.

Relationship dynamics

A further dimension of historical context which appeared important was the relationship of the students in this group. Sociodynamic perspectives on the construction of emotions underline the vital need to consider the continuing relationships in which certain interactional events (and corresponding emergence of emotions) are embedded (Boiger & Mesquita, 2015; Mesquita & Boiger, 2014). Boiger and Mesquita (2015) contend that:

> Individual meaning making is never a one-time process and does not occur in a social vacuum; rather, it is a social process through which people continuously integrate environmental information and, in doing so, update their emotional interpretations. ... Both the current relationship quality and future expectations for the relationship affect what emotions ensue.
>
> (p. 380)

Kazuma's group was together for 3 weeks, with the focal event occurring in the final week. Looking at the previous two weeks of dialogical data, it becomes apparent how little Kazuma spoke during lessons. Makito dominated – he was a stronger L2 user, had a pre-existing relationship with Wakana from other major classes at the university (Kazuma was in a different major cohort), and seemed to be trying to impress her. When first in this group (Lesson 9), Makito took over the conversation and group work, physically turned to face Wakana, and the two of them spoke and worked on exercises while Kazuma listened. Indeed, part of the reason for this group's overuse of Japanese in Lesson 10 was due to Makito's flirting. He tried to make Wakana laugh whenever possible, with Kazuma usually maintaining focus on any textbook exercise by himself rather than joining in. As one may guess, the flirting lead in directions which were, in the main, off-task. As an example, the following excerpt is from a video recording of Lesson 10. The interaction occurs while the rest of the class is working (rather vociferously!) together in their small groups on a written vocabulary exercise before a listening task. Seemingly triggered by one of the vocabulary items, Makito and Wakana are talking about the food in a particular country both had visited, as Kazuma completes the exercise alone (Table 7.2).

In contrast, by the third week of working together, the transcript reveals a very different picture. On the day of the significant emotional event for Kazuma, Wakana was quite apparently ill. She wore a face mask, her voice was muffled, and her actions were subdued. Throughout the first exchange of Kazuma and Makito (0:26–1:45), although Wakana turned toward the speakers, she made no attempt to contribute and sat unmoving with eyes glazed. She was on the fringes of the group. The serendipity of her illness seemed to abruptly alter the ongoing relationship dynamics, fostering a turning point not only through channeling the main contributors to the conversation but also Kazuma's emotions. In fact, similar findings of the impact of (chance) relationship dynamics connected with willingness to communicate in L2 groupwork were forthcoming in a study by Yashima (2021). In this longitudinal study, it was found that a certain learner frequently played a key role in fostering communication in the group. When this student was absent one day, it was presumed that discussion would be negatively impacted. In point of fact, however, the absence prompted other students to speak up more, resulting in the highest student talk ratio of any of the observed lessons (Yashima, 2021, p. 75). Looking at the transcript from the current study, while Kazuma still speaks less than Makito, by number of turns they are quite similar. Furthermore, consistent with his

Table 7.2 Transcript illustrating Makito and Wakana's relationship

Time	Name	Speech	Context / Emotion
0:00	M:	What do you think about the food there?	Looking at W, head up, sitting back; K working on textbook exercise
0:03	W:	I thought it was, so-so, I guess.	Laughs. M nods and laughs
0:08	M:	Yeah, it was very bad. *Maji mazukatta!* (It was so bad-tasting!)	Nodding.
0:10	W:	*Shio dake, deshou?* (It's just salt-flavored, isn't it?)	Tilts head – looking for agreement?
0:12	M:	*Un. Nanka, majide, ichiban umai no ha, hoteru no pan!* (Yeah. Like, honestly, the most delicious thing was the bread in the hotel!)	Nods. Looks at W, smiling. Head up
0:15	W:	*Pan!?*	M and W laughing. W eyebrows raised
0:16	M:	*Dake.* (That's all)	W laughs again; K looks up but seems uninterested

reflection that he "tried to speak first", the contributions that Kazuma makes on this day are qualitatively crucial to the continuation of the conversation.

In sum, the recent historical context of the teacher reminder to use English, Kazuma's not being able to talk much when first in this group – the "emotional baggage of learning" (Falout, 2016, p. 47) – along with the social context of Wakana being coincidentally sick on this day formed part of the landscape for the emergence of Kazuma's excited sense of progress.

Wider historical context

Widening the analytical lens to more distal reaches of the historical context further uncovers the interplay with past experiences and ongoing psychology that I termed Kazuma's "personality project".

Initial progress with a personality project

As noted, Kazuma, without exception, elected to "act positively" in the ideal classmates activity (Murphey et al., 2014; Murphey & Iswanti, 2014). In the second lesson of the semester, and the first in which these hopes were reintroduced to learners, his journal entry was almost entirely devoted to this ideal:

> I am so negative. However, I had decided to try one of Ideal classmates. I chose -Act positively. It request me participating in class actively. So I tried to speak with partners very well. Before speaking, I was afraid of partner's reaction but after speaking, I was so fun. I could talk with partners without problem. My challenge was a great success. I could tell partners about me and I could know about them. But I noticed. It is not easy to speak in English instantly. So, I will speak English more and I want to be able to speak in English fluently!
>
> (LJ, Week 2)

This extract reveals a good deal about interactions between Kazuma's ideas of his personality, actions in the classroom, emotions, L2 identity, and motivation. His understanding of personality is plainly stated from the start: "I am so negative". This conceptualization forms the motivation for his selection of the "act positively" ideal, which in turn prompted him to "tr[y] to speak with partners very well". Hence, we can begin to interpret Kazuma's own idea of his "negative" personality as being someone hesitant to interact with others. Anxiety connected with taking such a step is evident when he mentions that he "was afraid of partner's reaction" – a fundamental aspect of language anxiety for many (Gregersen & Horwitz, 2002; Horwitz et al., 1986). It is in the context of such long-term ideas of personality and anxious feelings that Kazuma experiences a profound sense of achievement in that he "could tell partners about me and I could know about them". As I have found previously (Sampson, 2019b), there is a bi-directional interaction between seemingly short-timescale aspects of emotion and longer timescale dimensions of personality: Kazuma's motivation to "act positively" is channeled by his unpleasant perceptions of personality, and it is in the context of such ongoing self-information that his success is surprising and rewarding. This emotionality would not have the same quality for a different person with different understandings of personality – the feeling is heavily afforded by his unique sensemaking (Feldman Barrett, 2018; Lemke, 2013).

As Witherington (2011) describes from a complexity perspective in reference to emergence, "a system's patterning is not merely an end product of more fundamental system process dynamics" but, rather, "such patterning itself contributes, by means of constraint, to the very processes that give rise to it" (p. 67). Further hints of such circular causality are importantly implicated near the end of Kazuma's entry: The ripple-effect back to his ideas of personality, while not overtly stated, seems apparent when he enthusiastically declares that "my challenge was a great success". Aligning with the findings of past research by Méndez López and Peña Aguilar (2013), amidst such a pleasant sense of accomplishment, his noticing of a gap in ability also prompts motivation to "speak English more", linking his excitement to an idea of a future L2 identity of being "able to speak in English fluently!" Thus, Kazuma's actions and emotions in the present are afforded by his ongoing (emotional) understandings of his psychology while these self-same actions and emotions in the present inform (emotional) ideas of his future (intentions, L2 identity, personality).

Feedback about a "negative" personality

Kazuma's personality project, hence, involved working on what he termed his "negative" personality, using the ideal classmates activity (Murphey et al., 2014) to try to act positively in lessons. As already hinted through writing in the previous extract, this dimension of his personality revolved around his propensity to withdraw in social situations. Again, pointing to general anxiety, a couple of lessons later he confided that:

> I decided to act positively again. ... I made an effort to talk with a person whom I had never spoken with. I reflect on this time because I couldn't speak well so that I was very nervous. I always have no confidence in myself. I can't believe myself and I worry to be ashamed.
>
> (LJ, Lesson 4)

While Kazuma details his specific effort to act positively during the lesson, his reflection is far less effusive than that regarding his "great success" in

Lesson 2. In a similar vein to the start of Tsutomu and Keiko's conversation in Chapter 4, it seems that the fact that his partner was "a person whom I had never spoken with" played a large part in eliciting unpleasant emotions. Yet, Kazuma's phrasing here is intriguing: While research into L2 classroom silence might encourage us to predict his noting of nervousness impeding his ability to speak (King & Smith, 2017; Smith & King, 2021), he reflects on quite the opposite. It appears that his perception that "I couldn't speak well" fostered anxiety, perhaps due to a self-imposed pressure through his intention to "make an effort to talk". Despite being possibly counterintuitive, MacIntyre's (2017) overview of years of language anxiety research aligns: "anxiety is both a result of problems encountered in the learning process and a cause of further difficulties" (p. 21). Unfortunately, although once more adding valuable qualitative detail to our picture of Kazuma's understandings of personality, his experiences on this day reinforce his existing conception: "I *always* have no confidence in myself. I can't believe myself and I worry to be ashamed" (emphasis added). That is, in the context of Kazuma's intention to change, his perceptions of failure seem representative of self-blame or shame, a "belief that [his] behavior, feelings, or actions do not meet [his] own standards, rules, and goals" (Oades-Sese et al., 2014, p. 251).

The development of patterns of complexity over time is a function of preceding states, with the possibility of becoming locked-in to a self-reinforcing feedback loop (Arthur, 1989). Current states and future potentialities are heavily dependent on past history (Juarrero, 2002). Such sensitivity implies that change in a radically different direction requires a large and/or consistent degree of energy (Arthur, 1989). It is, thus, impressive and gives a sense of the intensity of Kazuma's motivation to change that, even in the face of such feedback, he continued to select and try to "act positively" across the semester. (As a matter of fact, while Kazuma is quite harsh on himself, a different perspective is offered by his partner in this lesson, who mentioned: "My teammate spoke to me friendly too. So, I was really happy with that" [Keigo, LJ, Lesson 4]).

Agentic personality and emotions

As I mentioned at the start of this chapter, past research into the interactions between personality and L2 learning have been rather ambiguous (for overviews see e.g., Dewaele, 2013; Dörnyei & Ryan, 2015). Aligning with the cutting-edge research of Simsek and Dörnyei (2017), Kazuma's reflections suggest that one reason for the failure of past empirical work in this area could be an overly simplistic (Morin, 2008), reductive tendency to consider personality purely from the perspective of static traits: His writing clearly intimates a more agentic, unfolding view of personality in which he is consciously trying to act in ways different to how he sees himself currently limited. Moreover, emotional sensemaking of his actions in context feeds back to mold his ongoing conceptions, much like that proposed by McAdams and Pals' (2006) narrative identity dimension to personality. To put it bluntly, if we were to assign him the trait of being "introverted", we would be missing rather a lot of his story. Highlighting Kazuma's ongoing hope to alter this part of his personality and its connections with his L2 identity, in another entry the following week he reflected:

> I can't act as ideal positive man in my image yet. My ideal person talks loudly, clearly, easy to understand. In addition, he talks with others confidently. But in reality, I always hesitate. ... I have to have more confidence for me. ... We played dice game and talk about themes written on the board. It was very fun to listen to partner's various stories. I thought I wanted to talk to others more.
>
> (LJ, Lesson 5)

In fact, moving forward to the ninth lesson, upon joining his group with Makito and Wakana, Kazuma referred to Makito as "completely different from me" in his proactive and outgoing personality and, as such, "thought he was so cool". Kazuma's case hints at a non-linear relationship in the ways that personality and impressions of the personalities of others in communicative classroom settings interact with myriad psychological and social elements to foster (emotional) learning salients. Re-focusing back with a small lens on the significant emotional event in Lesson 11, he was able to become his "ideal positive man", "talk with others confidently", and *not* "always hesitate", perhaps even perceiving himself as "so cool", if for an instant. In this sense, his development over the semester appears to share some similarities with "fighters" in Simsek and Dörnyei's (2017) research into narrations of an "anxious self": Through his reflections and actions, Kazuma became more self-aware and active in re-narrating his personality. Nevertheless, it is only when we shine a light on the gradual build up in historical background that we can begin to understand the personal profoundness of his feeling of excitement and progress on the day in question.

Conclusion

Through looking at the sensemaking of Kazuma, I hope I have been able to achieve a more holistic appreciation of the development of emotions, their interactions with a multitude of other psychological and social aspects, and consequences for action and meaning. In particular, the current chapter pushed the long-term, ongoing intersections between personality and emotions to the fore. I openly admit, though, that my intention was always to maintain the small-lens focus on Kazuma's experience of *emotion*. Thus, centering more overtly on personality instead would no doubt reveal other, equally valid interpretations of his experiences over the semester. Nevertheless, I do contend that the representation I have constructed adds a more fluid, agentive understanding of personality intertwined with emotion.

The final two chapters take a look both backward and forward: backwards at what I hope can be learned from the new perspectives offered in this book and forward to potentialities in the future trajectory of researching and teaching connected to L2 study emotions.

8 Weaving threads for researching

At this point in my journey of exploring the emotionality of the people in my L2 classes, it seems apt to take stock of what I have learned and how it might be useful for others. Naturally, a first port of call in such a reckoning is to revisit the aim with which I set out. As the reader may recollect, in the opening chapter, I rendered the following intention for this book:

- To furnish more holistic yet detailed, social yet individual understandings of the emotions of people learning inside classrooms.

Moreover, I stated that my research and presentation of understandings would be underpinned by complexity thinking (Morin, 2008) while taking pains to not crowd the text with jargon for jargon's sake. Emergent from this philosophical grounding, I argued that:

- Complexity research requires a focus on real people in ecologically valid settings and takes a strong focus on dynamics and the ways in which phenomena evolve over time.

Any judgment as to how sufficiently I have achieved this aim and provided complex (yet not complicated!) interpretations of emotionality is ultimately the prerogative of the reader. Nevertheless, Chapters 8 and 9 set forth my own attempt to draw together the threads woven throughout the book into some kind of cohesive and useful pattern, with the current chapter centering on researching L2 study emotions.

The research presented in this text was essentially driven by my own curiosity about the seeming diversity of emotions I observed and interpreted learners as experiencing in my EFL classes. I was already relatively familiar with the empirical landscape of published work scrutinizing L2 study emotions. Notwithstanding, the selective review of more recent research presented in Chapter 2 established several areas in which scholars have pointed to the need for deeper understandings of emotions. In particular, it revealed gaps in consideration of the social emergence of emotions (Pavlenko, 2013) and ways to more sufficiently "capture" emotionality, including over intersecting timescales (Dewaele, 2021). While intertwined, it seems to make sense, then, to reflect on the contributions of the research in this book with regard to these areas.

Ways to sufficiently capture emotionality and the importance of social context

One of Dewaele's (2021) concerns with research to date and moving forward revolves around the ways in which we might reliably observe L2 study emotions. As he puts it, "because emotions cannot be measured directly, they are harder to capture and describe in an unequivocal way" (p. 208). Such a consideration is also foregrounded in Matthew Prior's (2016a) writing, which I quote at length here:

> Whereas researchers seek to measure and test emotions in accordance with scientific procedures, laypersons are more concerned with emotion as a means of apprehending and responding to the world and their place within it. To individuals going about the business of everyday life, it matters little that their anger at their boss, for example, is associated with low cerebral spinal fluid levels of 5-hydroxyindoleacetic acid ... or recurrent psychological stress in childhood. Neither are they likely to concern themselves with the fact that their delight at seeing a friend can be quantitatively substantiated by decreased heart rate, reduced muscle tension, or lower levels of skin-conductance ... For most people, it is sufficient that their emotions are recognized and acknowledged. On the practical level of everyday or "mundane" experience – where the communicative work of human life transpires – emotions matter in that they can be displayed, hidden, recognized, ascribed, contested, shared, responded to, or otherwise managed.
>
> (p. 4)

I feel that my position as a classroom practitioner striving to develop deeper understandings of the emotionality of my learners provides a natural balance between such "researcher" and "layperson" perspectives. In my case, what exactly we ought to "capture" and the ways of doing so when examining L2 study emotions revolves around whatever it is I hope, as a teacher, to understand more deeply. Although, as Prior (2016a) remarks, certain kinds of researchers may hold that measuring fluctuations in the make-up of cerebral spinal fluid or levels of skin-conductance offers valuable new insights into emotions, as a teacher, such dimensions are not practically useful. From my point of view, as someone working in education contexts, I wish, instead, to grasp a sense of *what* emotions my learners are experiencing and *how* these emotions appear to evolve and impact.

Which brings us to the second aspect of this section: A charge to render insights into emotions in social context (Pavlenko, 2013). As I introduced in Chapter 4, my thinking aligns with that of Ema Ushioda (2009, 2011) in considering that we need to delve into the emotions of people in-context and in-relation. A first response to Dewaele's (2021) question of ways to capture emotionality, therefore, concerns the setting: From a complexity perspective, in seeking to produce findings from research our "knowledge must be contextual" (Haggis, 2008, p. 158; see also Ushioda, 2015). If we are talking about L2 study emotions, it does not make sense to apply only techniques such as large-scale surveys that, by default, remove learners from any sense of their unique individual and social context. As Atkinson (2019) questions in an article arguing strongly for a focus in SLA studies on the "ecosocial": "Are human environments not ... pervasively social – that is, does our embodied adaptive action not depend crucially on social action and cooperation with others? ... Is such social action/cooperation ultimately not what language and language learning are for?" (p. 726). We ought to explore emotions *as* they emerge *in* their contexts of emergence – in the social sites of learning for real people.

While the specific settings differed, in Chapters 4–7, I offered interpretations that might allow the reader to feel as if they were right there, with these participants, in the particular interactional context of the classroom. I applied Ushioda's (2016) proposal of taking a "small lens" approach, which, once more, provides responses to the questions of this section. In the small-lens approach, we home in on significant emotional episodes and examine the interplay of internal psychological processes with external contextual elements of the social setting. In the work presented in this book, I used reflective journals to illuminate the internal and video recording to furnish the external. My analysis clearly revealed that emotions have dimensions more sufficiently uncovered via asking learners to tell us what they are feeling (Damasio, 2003) and other aspects that are, in many ways, observable as part of behaviors in a social context (Reisenzein et al., 2014). By converging on only one or the other of these angles, we will miss a good deal of the emotional stories of our learners. Take the case of Tsutomu and Keiko presented in Chapter 4: If I had purely examined the external (video of interactions), I would have had no idea of the impact the conversation had on these learners' overall experience of the lesson on that day. Alternatively, if I had, instead, investigated only the internal (reflections), the seemingly trivial, self-organizing qualities of these students' interactions through which such an important outcome arose would have been lost. It is via iteratively pivoting between these aspects that we can work to afford more subtle and phenomenological depictions of emotions, their emergence, and their impact.

There will be some who may wonder as to the significance of any findings generated or implications emergent from centering on limited cases and only specific, emotionally significant events (e.g., Ellis, 2021; Pallotti, 2021). Questions may also be raised by those who follow a stricter conversation analytical or discursive psychology approach that only admits the observable (e.g., Prior, 2016; Wiggins, 2017). Some "third-party researchers" from outside teaching contexts who especially "seek to develop or refine our theoretical understandings" (Ushioda, 2021, p. 274) might also have concerns relating to the localized, practitioner-research nature of the setup of the study and the potential for bias in participants "writing for the teacher". However, I hope to have shown the possibility that the selection by a key player in the learning context – myself as teacher – and merging of perspectives on a single event or shared experience brings us closer to a more phenomenological understanding of L2 learner psychology with practical implications. Indeed, Amerstorfer (2020) found that taking such a focused perspective underpinned by complexity principles allowed her to uncover more "wide-ranging processes and trigger[ed] complex considerations and intricate reasoning" (p. 37) regarding one of her students. She concluded that a fine focus in classroom research:

> can have practical benefits for students' EFL development because it intertwines multiple strands of dynamic, situational information and hence enables conclusions of practical relevance. Informed by complexity studies, teachers can act upon their students' problems.
>
> (p. 38)

In short, through shifting our focus on different angles, we might afford a more detailed glimpse of the emergence of emotions for each L2 learner as a "real person, with real hopes, fears, worries, joys, disappointments, thrills and mistakes" (Taylor, 2013, p. 126).

There are without doubt other possibilities for how we might additionally gain nuanced pictures of L2 study emotions in a social context. As described in Chapter 2, Pawlak et al. (2021) combined questionnaires, a grid filled out at 5-minute intervals during lessons, and written reflections to unearth a dynamic picture of L2 study boredom. MacIntyre's (2012) idiodynamic method has made use of video recordings and stimulated recall with participants to focus on the situated ebb and flow of willingness to communicate (MacIntyre & Legatto, 2011), language anxiety (Gregersen et al., 2014), and language anxiety and enjoyment (Boudreau et al., 2018).[1]

Equally, championed by Prior (e.g., Prior, 2016, 2019; Prior & Kasper, 2016), there are increasing calls in applied linguistics research to center on the expressed, displayed, and pragmatic utility of emotions in discourse via forms of conversation analysis and discursive psychology. As Prior (2016a) contests, "what have frequently escaped analytical attention are the ways in which emotion gets produced, displayed, oriented to, and managed by interactants in the midst of their ongoing activities" (p. 2). Such a focus is certainly on display in his edited volume (Prior & Kasper, 2016), with Gonzalez-Lloret's (2016) contribution especially providing a useful counterpoint to my own work on L2 online chat (Sampson & Yoshida, 2020) by concentrating purely on "how emotion is made available to other participants in the interaction" (p. 291).

Another potential avenue to extend both research understandings and methods of representation that might do more justice to the multidimensional nature of emotions is multimodal analysis (e.g., Goodwin, 2000, 2010, 2018; Norris, 2004, 2011, 2020). Like any area of inquiry, the breadth of this field is truly impressive, and I must admit that I am only just beginning to make my own way into exploring the landscape. As such, the reader is advised to consult any of the works I have cited for a more worthy description. In essence, multimodal analysis involves examining the ways in which interactions evolve over various intertwining communicative modes. These communicative modes encompass anything from spoken language, proximity, posture, gesture, head movements, gaze, print, and even layout (or the setting and objects therein) (Norris, 2004). The observer selects a short (30–40 second) interaction of interest, usually recorded by video camera. They then work to produce a description that gives insight into how the coalescence of modes contribute to the interaction – or in regard to the focus of this book, how the emotionality of interactants emerges. Although there are different manners of representation, Norris' method includes a timestamped series of freeze-frames with spoken elements posted directly on top of each frame. An interpretation is added that refers to these different points in time and their role in the interaction. As Norris (2004) thus reminds:

> The task of a multimodal transcript is not to analyze the images that are incorporated, but rather to use the images to describe the dynamic unfolding of specific moments in time, in which the layout and modes like posture, gesture, and gaze play as much a part as the verbal.
>
> (p. 65)

Considering the small-lens approach (Ushioda, 2016) I took to exploring the emergence of significant emotional episodes in this book, it would seem that a multimodal analysis might offer much in terms of adding visual grounding to any interpretation. While I endeavored to furnish sufficient details to transcripts of social interactions by including written descriptions of such elements as posture, gaze, and movements, freeze-frames of the interaction itself would instantly convey such embodied dimensions. Whether more inclined toward conversation analysis, discursive psychology, or multimodal analysis, as I remarked in introducing my own style of transcription in the current work, I would, nevertheless, urge researchers to strive to make their representations accessible to the people for whom they might be useful – practitioners in classrooms.

Consideration of timescales

A challenge identified by MacIntyre et al., (2021) for research into the psychology of L2 learners is to "combine research examining systems at various levels of granularity and across timescales" (p. 30). In order to deepen understandings of L2 emotionality, consideration of *which* timescales might be most profitably focused upon has also been positioned as crucial (Dewaele, 2021).

A timescale relates to the temporal granularity with which we explore a process (de Bot, 2015). From a complexity perspective, de Bot (2015) urges that "we cannot undo the interaction between timescales and study phenomena on one timescale without taking into account other timescales" (p. 36). There is a tendency to think of the focus of emotions as linked to an event or object purely in the present acting as a "trigger" and, thus, of emotions themselves as "instantaneous" or "momentary" (Feldman Barrett & Russell, 2015). In contrast, as I touched upon in Chapter 1, theories of constructed emotion consider that people's brains play a far more proactive role in creating instances of emotion-as-meaning (Boiger & Mesquita, 2015; Feldman Barrett, 2018; Russell, 2015). As Russell (2015) comments:

> Like all perceptions, emotional meta-experiences are interpretations. The raw data on which the interpretation is based are both top-down (e.g., concepts, stored knowledge, expectations, attributions, appraisals, and memories) and bottom-up (from both the internal world via somatosensory feedback and the external world).
>
> (p. 195)

That is, our emotions do not follow a simplistic, linear "external stimulus triggers internal psychological process triggers response" pattern (Feldman Barrett, 2015). We need to contemplate interactions between our present – the "bottom-up" – and pertinent past experiences and knowledge – the "top-down" (Russell, 2015). In parallel with ideas of development from complexity perspectives, up to the point in time at which we observe it, a phenomenon, such as emotion, emerges through the accumulation of dynamics in numerous interrelated, nested systems (de Wolf & Holvoet, 2005; Witherington, 2011). As one aspect of considering such nested dynamics, I have previously argued that examination of the intersections between different timescales might be facilitative in affording a phenomenological interpretation of the emergence of L2 study emotions (Sampson, 2019b, 2021).

In a related vein, complexity perspectives remind us of the open nature of the psychological and social phenomena we are observing. We live forming and formed by a multitude of nested contexts (Bronfenbrenner, 1979). Any definition of boundaries to these contexts is somewhat arbitrary, with the range of our interest instead determined by the purpose of description of the observer (Cilliers, 1998). Van Lier (2004) argues the necessity to remain cognizant of the openness of the classroom (or any learning context) and the experiences of the people therein:

> The learners spend an hour or so in the classroom, but before that they have been elsewhere, and after that they will go to other places. There is no doubt that their activities elsewhere have an effect on what happens in the classroom, and the same naturally goes for the teacher. Classroom research … has often treated the classroom as a bounded system, and studied the interactions and language in it without explicit connections to other contexts.
>
> (p. 194)

In education research, we must, thus, aim to "encompass the totality of the relationships that a learner, as a living organism, entertains with all aspects of his/her environment" (Kramsch, 2002, p. 22). In the dynamic emergence of motivation for his L2 learners, Consoli (2021) uncovered a complex interplay between what he terms life story (life as it unfolds for a human being, situated in societal, institutional, and political structures) and life capital (memories, desires, emotions, attitudes, and opinions). Indeed, my own past research with learners in a senior-high school setting revealed their motivation and ideas of L2 self (Dörnyei, 2009) to be intricately intertwined with numerous nested contexts not constrained to the L2 class: aspects of the college timetabling and exams, past schooling experiences, current personal life, very general societal messages about the L2 in Japan, and even the time of day and the seasons (!) (Sampson, 2016).

The interaction of timescales and openness has likewise been on display throughout the empirical chapters of this book. In Chapter 3, even the more generalized, broad-brush description of the kinds of emotions experienced by students in my class revealed differences across lesson segments. The multiple threading provided a visual reminder that emotionality in any particular lesson is located in the midst of personalized emotional narratives over a semester. The small-lens approach (Ushioda, 2016) I utilized in Chapters 4–7 then uncovered a more nuanced picture of the emergence of emotional meaning over intertwining timescales. Emotionality was situated at one and the same time in instances of social interaction and even more finely in particular utterances or other communicative modes (e.g., vocal bursts such as "O::h" combined with nodding as interested recognition of a shared piece of knowledge); in the developing and fluctuating relationships of learners (e.g., "flirting" that excluded Kazuma giving way to involvement because of Wakana's chance illness); in the lesson-sequence in the semester (e.g., having worked or not with a partner, having been "admonished" the previous lesson to use more of the L2, being busy because of numerous assignments); and in the specific moment in more general historical time (as when discussion of the YouTuber "Hikaru" had special significance at that point in time because of his contentious actions, or the music group Perfume being widely popular). The emotions of learners were also co-adaptive (Larsen-Freeman & Cameron, 2008) across longer timescales still, as with ideas of personality and how it impacted actions and (emotional) interpretations of actions, yet also engendered agency to change; dimensions of learners' ongoing beliefs about appropriate and facilitative actions in learning contexts; and their evolving identities as not only (L2) learners but as students in general, people with their own interests and agendas and lives (e.g., being fans of Studio Ghibli, knowing the particular songs of a pop group or particular YouTubers).

I would, thus, propose a partial response to Dewaele's (2021) entreaty: Rather than determining, in any generalized way at the outset, specific timescales upon which to focus, the interpretations of my students' emotions presented in this book have brought me to an understanding that the question of, "Which timescales?" might most usefully be answered in the course of analysis. If we take emotions as sensed and having meaning for particular people in particular contexts at particular times, we need to heed *their* definition of timescales, not those pre-supposed by researchers or theorists. A natural implication of emphasizing *research participants'* experience of emotions as "active engagements[,] ... meanings", and "signifiers of something more" (Lemke, 2013, p. 84) is that we do, however, need to collect data in ways that allow the interaction of timescales to become usefully apparent.

Conclusion

In the current chapter, I have summarized my thinking about suggestions for further empirical work grounded in my experiences with the study that forms the basis of this book. In this regard, I structured the chapter around my responses to some of the tasks for future research delineated by the previous body of literature (see Chapter 2) – in particular the questions of how most usefully to capture emotions in L2 learning, the sociality of their emergence, and the interactions between timescales in their evolution.

The final chapter presents my ideas related to my "other" (and perhaps main) identity in my working life – what I have learned from this research that I deem informative for my own future pedagogical practice and, hopefully, that of others also.

Note

1 I find the idiodynamic method offers great potential in uncovering the dynamicity of L2 learner (and teacher) psychology. Rather than being a third-person interpretation (as I must admit my own empirical work to be), the idiodynamic method allows the experiencers themselves to give voice to their own experience of different aspects of their psychology and sociality. The idiodynamic method also, thus, allows the researcher to really focus in on moments of interest and ask about them specifically. I must admit that my own use of journals is inferior in this regard – there are certainly times when I find something interesting or hinted at in this data, yet the participant has not naturally expanded on that topic. At the same time, as a classroom practitioner-researcher teaching undergraduates in compulsory L2 courses, I do also have ethical reservations about the idiodynamic method: Practitioner-researchers aim to interweave data collection as much as possible with regular classroom activities. In my own context, I would not like to add to the already busy lives of my students the burden of asking them to – outside class time – deliberate while watching the video recording of their interactions and then, on top of this, interview them about their interpretations. In this, I recognize that I am highly influenced by the context in which I find myself teaching – my students are, in the main, *not* language majors but are (to be blunt) simply ticking the box of studying the required quota of additional language courses. Additionally, Japanese undergraduates in their first or second year of tertiary study are typically obliged to take between 14 to 18 classes per week, each lasting 90–100 minutes. Many of my learners, moreover, work part-time jobs to pay for their everyday expenses. They would simply not have the time (or, most likely, the energy!) to add to their already hectic lives and pore over their experiences to the degree necessary in the idiodynamic method. Hence, I feel it would be an ethical abuse of my power over them as a teacher to even ask.

9 Pedagogy for emotionally charged educational spaces

As I have stressed throughout this book, my intentions in conducting the research contained herein revolved around understanding the people in my classes more deeply. As a practitioner-researcher, I feel it is imperative that what I have learned will have practical utility for my own pedagogical practice going forward and may also resonate with other practitioners.

In my teaching practice and research, I align with the underpinnings of complexity thinking (Morin, 2008). Around a decade before writing this book, Sarah Mercer (2013) offered to my mind one of the most facilitative attempts at describing a pedagogy informed by complexity principles. Adapting and adding to Mercer's (2013) guiding principles for practice with insights from my own past classroom-based research (Sampson, 2016a), as teachers, we might strive to:

- Be flexible and adaptive.
- Be sensitive to the dynamics in the classroom.
- Embrace individual diversity.
- Value and promote human relationships via chances to communicate personally meaningful identities.
- Recognize that teachers and learners co-contribute to effective classroom life.
- Foster quality learning *processes* and *opportunities*.

Various of these principles will make their flavors known as I reflect on the pedagogical implications of the research contained in this book. Nevertheless, I am also aware that the feasibility of implementing any recommendations I make will be impacted by a myriad of local teaching concerns, including simply being too busy with any current content. In this regard, I concur with Mercer's (2013) important caveat:

While these principles can help educators to reflect on the possible nature of and dynamics of their classrooms, they can never, and are not intended to, provide specific answers to the particular challenges facing individual classrooms nor are they intended to prescribe a supposed "ideal" universal form of pedagogy. Instead ... it is hoped that they may serve as guiding principles or simply food for thought for others. Ultimately, each "messy" and unique classroom will require its own local teaching strategies and procedures as appropriate for its individual composition and settings.

(p. 395)

Diversity and constancy of emotionality

The majority of this book centers on specific, significant emotional episodes from which I myself could learn about the people sharing my L2 study contexts, and from which I feel others also may be able to deepen their understandings. However, while focusing on such cases, I do not wish to downplay the emotionality of all learners. As the multiple threading in Chapter 3 reminds, L2 study contexts are profoundly emotional spaces. Aligning with neuroscientific research (e.g., Immordino-Yang, 2016), the multiple threading furnishes a visual reminder of the colorful canvas of emotion interwoven throughout all learners' experiences in the classroom. Such a representation additionally calls attention to the intricate diversity of emotional experience for individuals, even within the same activity, across lesson segments, or spanning a semester of study. Regardless, as teachers, I feel that such emotionality often flows past us, lost as we focus (or are directed to focus) on cognitive learning progress and outcomes. Instead of such instrumentality, we must remind ourselves that "learning is an activity valuable for its own sake even though it has goals", and recognize that "time at school is a lived human experience and is an important part of a young person's current life" (Gill & Thomson, 2017, p. 3). Based on the research in this book, I hope (and would urge other teachers) to remain cognizant of the brilliant emotional landscape that the members of any learning group co-form as part of these lived experiences.

Reflecting on an emotional void – textbook segments of my lessons

In light of such apparent diversity and constancy, we might also reflect on the emotional quality of experiences as learners spend time on their education. For instance (to step outside the bounds of the current study for a moment), as part of a project-based EFL course with undergraduates majoring in education, I recently inquired with students in my classes as to their fondest memories of time in primary and secondary schooling. While learners discussed in groups, I listened in to get a feel for the kinds of experiences about which they were reflecting. I then asked them to write a short paragraph concerning these memories (which afterward formed the basis for one of their projects about revising the education system here in Japan). Looking at the reflections of more than 70 learners, not a single "fond memory" centered on explicit study experiences. Episodes at school sports festivals, spending time with class friends during excursions or graduation trips, the relationships formed via school (sports) club activities, or gaining experience as part of a large-scale brass band (relatively common in Japan) all featured heavily. Yet none of these students, the majority of whom will become teachers themselves in the future, reminisced about "fond memories" related to study or developing their academic knowledge and abilities.

Returning to the research in this book, a similar state of affairs is hinted at in the analysis in Chapter 3. Some segments of lessons (the short conversation sessions and humanistic activities) witnessed an outpouring of a diverse range of references to emotion from my learners. Yet, in sharp contrast, considering the proportion of time devoted to textbook study (usually around two-fifths to a half of each lesson), students' reflections revealed this segment to be a relative emotional wasteland. Significantly, especially in comparison with the short conversation sessions (which lasted between a mere 2 to 8 minutes), the scarcity of emotional references related to work with the textbook is stark. This impoverishment is all the more disappointing considering that the textbook listening exercises were a core element of the compulsory curriculum at this university. The textbook segment of lessons witnessed not only less reference to emotions but also a more subdued palette of emotions.

Founded on my past experiences teaching such courses, I had, to a degree, anticipated challenges in engagement connected with the textbook segments of lessons. The extra textbook activities that extended the featured listening skills while drawing on elements of my own and students' identities as other than teacher or learner at times elicited more emotional references from students (Chapter 3). Looking forward to both my own and other teachers' practice with textbook portions of lessons, we might consult any one of the many webpages, online presentations, and instructional books that abound concerning strategies to adapt commercial textbooks. Another possibility would be to utilize what Pinner (2019) has referred to as "the living textbook" rather than a commercially available product – a set of pedagogical materials "constantly being updated, adapted and altered for each class, to fit the individuals that make up a class as a whole" (p. 117).

Regardless, one of the leading researchers of emotions in education importantly summarizes that "emotions control students' attention, influence their motivation to learn, modify the choice of learning strategies, and affect their self-regulation of learning" (Pekrun, 2014, p. 6). In response, the emergence of an emotional void connected with textbook exercises for learners strongly suggests a need for teachers to find ways to adapt content to connect more (constructively) with students' emotions.

Pleasant ≠ positive, unpleasant ≠ negative

Within the field of L2 teaching and research, there is increasing appreciation of the potential of looking at more positive dimensions of students' psychologies and experiences (see volume edited by MacIntyre, Gregersen, & Mercer, 2016). Rather than concentrating on "problematic, distressing aspects that have often been psychology's centerpiece", a positive-psychology approach to education "looks at positive elements and strengths in the human psyche and human experience" (Oxford, 2016, p. 11) and how these relate to actions and learning. This widening of scope may have developed in part in reaction to the longstanding fascination with language anxiety (Horwitz et al., 1986) and especially via newer research into language enjoyment (Boudreau et al., 2018; Dewaele & Alfawzan, 2018; Dewaele & MacIntyre, 2014, 2016).

However, we must resist the simplistic temptation to equate pleasant emotions with the positive and unpleasant emotions with the negative. As Pinner (2016) points out based on his own practitioner research, "not all learning experiences have to be *good*. In fact, some of the best learning experiences come from *bad* experiences and these have an important contribution to make in both education and learning" (p. 182). In outlining her breathtaking "EMPATHICS" vision of well-being for language learners, Oxford (2016) is quite explicit in stressing that "positive psychology, with its concentration on well-being, does not ignore human difficulties, but it faces them from the point of view of human strength rather than weakness" (p. 11). Indeed, a range of past work has found that unpleasant emotions such as anger, sadness, anxiety, failure, disappointment, and a sense of difficulty can serve as wake-up calls to take specific action (Dewaele & MacIntyre, 2014; Imai, 2010; Méndez López & Peña Aguilar, 2013; Oxford, 2014; Oxford et al., 2007; Sampson, 2019b, 2020; Simsek & Dörnyei, 2017; Ushioda, 2011b).

I am certainly not arguing that I wish learners in my classrooms to experience unpleasant emotions consistently or with more intensity than pleasant emotions. Rather, the research in this book attests to the fact that the unpleasant can (in some cases) prompt learners to explore different behaviors, expanding the range of the possible. Viewed from the perspective of complexity, negative feedback suggests a particular behavior to be inappropriate for the situation and that the chances of adaptive actions will increase (Byrne & Callaghan, 2014). There are clearly such cases on display in the examples in this book: For instance, Akito (Chapter 6) recognizing the difference in possibilities for his actions and sensemaking with different group members, and Kazuma (Chapter 7) finding an opportunity not only for reflection but also to act to change long-held ideas about his personality.

Based on my interpretations of the emotions of the young people in my classes, I feel that one major step to providing a more productive emotional footing to language education is to incorporate opportunities for noticing emotions rather than merely letting them wash over and away. As the voices of participants in one of my previous studies chorused, learners have too few chances for reflecting on and thinking about themselves (Sampson, 2016a). To this end, classroom activities, like those described by Murphey (2021), that prompt students to consider themselves and their ways of learning and growing from different angles are immediately facilitative. Although seemingly not as beneficial in the context of the research presented in Chapter 7, interventions with learners acting on images of ideal classmates have been shown to allow all those in a class group to consider both their own and others' behaviors (and linked emotions) (Murphey et al., 2014; Sampson, 2018). Pondering specifically the episodes in this book, teachers may build opportunities for learners to discuss their emotional experiences and share ideas for building a more facilitative emotional environment with their peers. Although in the different contexts of online chat, direct discussion of emotional scaffolding strategies, such as those emergent in Yoshida's (2020) research, may also prove facilitative. Particularly considering what we can learn from Akito's story in Chapter 6, if learners had in-class time to share their perceptions, teachers and peers may be able to guide them to step away from experiences and make more constructive sense of them. As Kazuma's story in Chapter 7, moreover, clearly illustrates, it appears that having opportunities to look back on experiences, to reframe and re-narrate, can play a vital role in nudging ideas of unpleasant emotional episodes in more constructive directions (see also work in this area connected with L2 learning by Dufva & Aro, 2015; Falout, 2016; Simsek & Dörnyei, 2017). Finally, additional, situated case studies might also deepen our understandings of potential conditions in which unpleasant emotions engender constructive or unconstructive propensities, with the hope that such research may concretely contribute to allowing teachers to better support the students in our classes.

Transportable identities

In the slightly different realm of L2 *motivation* research, Ushioda (2020) has argued convincingly that:

> In our approaches to theorizing language learning motivation, we all too easily forget that the "subjects" of our theorizing are uniquely individual people, with all their complex micro-diversity and macro-diversity, who are engaging with the world with multiple motivations across multiple areas of learning, and who are located in particular physical, historical, cultural, social, and even virtual realities. They are not just "language learners", who are narrowly defined and positioned by this L2 learning identity that we impose on them. Rather, they are people who happen to be learning a language, among other things, in their busy lives, and who are engaging in this process with varying motivations and motivational experiences.
>
> (p. 42)

In concurrence, across the introspective and dialogical data in this book, analysis revealed little sense that the participants are "L2 learners" with only L2-specific emotions. They are young people discussing what has meaning for them, and they happen to be doing it through an L2. Of course, my own choice to focus on the limited situation of the short conversation segment of lessons exacerbated this occurrence of participants interacting on their own terms. Nevertheless, examining dialogical data opened a window on the ways in which learners' emotions are situated in their dynamically fluid interactions as they engage their transportable identities (Zimmerman, 1998) and "be and become themselves" (Ushioda, 2009, p. 223) through the L2. As the examples showed, such short or seemingly trivial opportunities can also be pivotal in engendering pleasant experience of a lesson as a whole (e.g., Chapters 4 and 5). While somewhat different from drawing specific, non-situated *identities* into the linguistic and emotional landscape of classroom interactions (Zimmerman, 1998), Kazuma's story (Chapter 7) also highlights the ways in which transported understandings and expressions of *personality* co-adaptively inform action and emotionality.

As I have reflected upon in past explorations of the emergence of my own emotions and motivations as a teacher (Sampson, 2016a, b, 2022), transportable identities and personality are equally involved in teacher self-disclosure. In essence, teacher self-disclosure involves "statements in the classroom about the self that may or may not be related to the subject content, but reveal information about the teacher that students are unlikely to learn from other sources" (Sorenson, 1989). Such teacher self-disclosure has been found to interact with a range of constructive educational processes, such as enhancing attention to and understanding of content, and fostering enjoyment, interest, and engagement (see Elahi Shirvan & Taherian, 2021 for a concise review). I am sure that most teachers can recall times when we have been surprised and overwhelmed at how our introduction of transportable identities to the classroom is received: I clearly remember one such occasion when my (at that time still very young) children had implored me to show the fledgling engineers in my university classes some quite bizarre Lego constructions. My students not only kindly praised these contraptions, but after returning home, some of them even made their own models and presented me with photographs to show my children. Needless to say, I was moved!

However, we (teachers or learners) may equally "take a chance" and draw in to the classroom one of our personally important identities, yet find the "energy return on our investment" (Pinner, 2016b, 2019) is not only lacking but feel affronted at having shared ourselves only to be met with disinterest. Such an occurrence is clearly apparent in Pinner's (2019) classroom research, during which a personal incident (an extreme bicycle accident) was met with sympathy – and resultant "motivational synergy" – by one group of students, while another group of students revealed no indications of caring (pp. 202–203). Indeed, as Richards (2006) has cautioned, drawing on transportable identities "may have the power to transform the sort of interaction that takes place in the classroom", but it will also "involve an investment of self, with all the emotional, relational, and moral considerations that this invokes" (p. 72). In the example case in Chapter 5, the students naturally expressed emotional intersubjectivities (Denzin, 1984) that relieved anxiety and hesitancy in broaching personally important identities. However, such a process may certainly not occur spontaneously in all cases in terms of learners and teachers. Indeed, in spite of moves to locate identity as fundamental to L2 learning (e.g., Dörnyei & Ushioda, 2009; Miyahara, 2015; Murray et al., 2011; Norton, 2000), Ushioda (2020) reminds that learners in contexts in which L2 learning is compulsory may, in fact, not wish to connect other important aspects of their lives to L2 learning. There is clearly a need for caution in encouraging other teachers to create opportunities for learners to draw in their transportable identities without discretion. We must give our learners the choice of what and how much they transport into and share with any learning group.

Sociality of emotions/emotional intersubjectivities

One of the primary (empirical) contributions of this book is a more situated glimpse of the ways in which L2 learners' emotionality emerges in social context via their communicative interactions. In this regard, I am reminded of the oft-remarked-upon truism that "teaching is an impossible enterprise". A mechanic fixes something such as a car, a truck driver transports goods from one location to another, a doctor diagnoses and prescribes regimens of treatment in order for patients to regain their health. In many occupations, people can be relatively confident of intended outcomes. While, as teachers, we can occasion certain opportunities for development, as I have remarked previously, "the direction and quality of learning is ultimately co-formed with and between all members of the class group" (Sampson, 2016a, p. 7). A teacher cannot ensure learning; we cannot *make* a learner learn, despite out best intentions and plans.

The cases described in the previous chapters illustrate that this is equally true for the emotional experiences of the learners in our classrooms. In the context of occasioned learning activities and everything occurring in their (psychological) lives, it is via the social interactions of students that emotional experience of learning spaces emerges. Although I was aware of these processes to a degree (as I presume all teachers must be), the small-lens (Ushioda, 2016) perspective gave me a much clearer view of the fine evolution of L2 study emotions. I could never have predicted the qualities of emotional experiences given voice in these chapters – the large impact on emotional experience of a lesson as a whole based on a 1-minute communicative interaction (Chapter 4); the development of pleasant emotional inter-subjectivities (Denzin, 1984) via a discussion of YouTube and pop-singers, in fact, based on experiences of disappointment (Chapter 5); the constructive subjective interpretation of anxiety founded in comparisons with previous experiences (Chapter 6); the focused uptake by one student of the ideal classmates activity (Murphey et al., 2014) and his critical experience of a sense of progress in adapting personality, all located in social interactions enabled via another student being serendipitously ill (Chapter 7). As a teacher, such insights are both inspiring and perhaps a little intimidating.

It goes without saying that most formal L2 learning spaces involve peer-to-peer social interactions. While it has been pointed out that language professionals, learners, and researchers alike understand the limitations of peer interactions in terms of focus on L2 grammaticality or the probability of corrective feedback, such opportunities are also seen as a more "egalitarian context for practice" (Philp et al., 2014, pp. 197–198). Synthesizing a large body of research into peer interaction and L2 language learning, Philp et al. (2014) conclude that such peer social interactions not only afford more "emotional salience" for learners, but additionally "provide a 'safe' space to try out language, to take risks, to have fun with language, and to experiment and make mistakes without worrying about 'being right'" (p. 199). However, in the context of such unscripted social interactions, if emotionality is largely self-organizing and emergent (Larsen-Freeman & Cameron, 2008), how can teachers work to facilitate the likelihood of more constructive emotional trajectories?

A running theme across chapters was the social affirmation of relatedness (Ryan & Deci, 2002, 2017) in discussing shared interests and my interpretations of the development of emotional embracement (Denzin, 1984) as a kind of shared emotionality. In many ways, it seems that emotional embracement in a formal L2 study situation might occur by chance – the chance that learners interact around some topic that has shared personal meaning for them. Notwithstanding, such processes are quite different in quality to what Denzin (1984) terms "spurious emotionality", in which "individuals mistake their own feelings for the feelings of the other and interpret their feelings as the feelings of the other" (p. 154). In this regard, teachers may wish to explore the use of the Managing Your Emotions questionnaire (see Oxford & Gkonou, 2021), which would allow learners to consider their (L2 study) emotions and, importantly, their (social) emotion regulation strategies. Such an endeavor could possibly raise student awareness of how their own actions and emotional displays might be interpreted by others while also suggesting ways to regulate their emotions in interactions. If everyone in a class took the questionnaire, they could then discuss together the different situations, which might also, in itself, allow opportunities for the development of emotional embracement. It is, moreover, a question for future, small-lens research as to ways in which facilitative emotional intersubjectivities emerge in L2 study contexts and how they can be further fostered.

In closing

As I arrive at the end of this particular journey with a handful of ideas for heading forward, yet with still more questions, I am reminded of one of the key lessons I learned from a 16-year-old secondary school participant in one of my previous practitioner studies: That, at the very least, I have grown and that "now, there is a me who is doing his best" to interpret and understand the L2 study emotions of my learners, and "even just through that, it's different from the me before" (Taku, from Sampson, 2016a, p. 185).

Appendix

Transcription conventions (Adapted and abridged from Jefferson, 2004; Prior, 2016)

(1.2)	A pause or silence, measured in seconds and tenths of seconds
=	Latched talk, during which there is no hearable gap between words
::	Prolonged sounds – the more colons, the longer the sound
word	Emphasized words or parts of words
?	Rising intonation (may be a question, but not necessarily)
((description))	Details about additional descriptions
tango	Japanese word (followed on first occurrence by translation in parenthesis)
[]	Start and end of overlapping talk
wor°	A word cut off
°word or phrase°	Whispered word or phrase

References

Amerstorfer, C. M. (2020). The dynamism of strategic learning: Complexity theory in strategic L2 development. *Studies in Second Language Learning and Teaching, 10*(1), 21–44.

Arnold, J., & Brown, D. H. (1999). A map of the terrain. In J. Arnold (Ed.), *Affect in language learning* (pp. 1–24). Cambridge University Press.

Arthur, B. (1989). Competing technologies, increasing returns, and lock-in by historical events. *Economic Journal, 99*, 116–131.

Atkinson, D. (2019). Beyond the brain: Intercorporeality and co-operative action for SLA studies. *The Modern Language Journal, 103*(4), 724–738.

Baumgartner, H., Pieters, R., & Bagozzi, R. P. (2008). Future-oriented emotions: Conceptualization and behavioral effects. *European Journal of Social Psychology, 38*(4), 685–696.

Bazeley, P. (2013). *Qualitative data analysis: Practical strategies*. Sage.

Bodine, E., & Kramsch, C. (2002). Part one commentaries. In C. Kramsch (Ed.), *Language acquisition and language socialization: Ecological perspectives* (pp. 88–95). Continuum.

Boiger, M., & Mesquita, B. (2012). The construction of emotions in interactions, relationships, and cultures. *Emotion Review, 4*(3), 221–229.

Boiger, M., & Mesquita, B. (2015). A sociodynamic perspective on the construction of emotion. In L. Feldman Barrett & J. A. Russell (Eds.), *The psychological construction of emotion* (pp. 377–398). Guilford Press.

Boudreau, C., MacIntyre, P. D., & Dewaele, J.-M. (2018). Enjoyment and anxiety in second language communication: An idiodynamic approach. *Studies in Second Language Learning and Teaching, 8*(1), 149–170.

Bronfenbrenner, U. (1979). *The ecology of human development*. Harvard University Press.

Byrne, D., & Callaghan, G. (2014). *Complexity theory and the social sciences: The state of the art*. Routledge.

Cahour, B. (2013). Emotions: Characteristics, emergence and circulation in interactional learning. In M. Baker, J. Andriessen, & S. Jarvela (Eds.), *Affective learning together: Social and emotional dimensions of collaborative learning* (pp. 52–70). Routledge.

References

Cilliers, P. (1998). *Complexity and postmodernism: Understanding complex systems*. Routledge.

Consoli, S. (2021). Understanding motivation through ecological research: The case of exploratory practice. In R. J. Sampson & R. S. Pinner (Eds.), *Complexity perspectives on researching language learner and teacher psychology* (pp. 120–135). Multilingual Matters.

Cordaro, D. T., Keltner, D., Tshering, S., Wangchuk, D., & Flynn, L. M. (2016). The voice conveys emotion in ten globalized cultures and one remote village in Bhutan. *Emotion, 16*(1), 117–128.

Council of Europe. (2001). *Common European framework of reference for languages: Learning, teaching, assessment*. Cambridge University Press.

Damasio, A. (2003). *Looking for Spinoza: Joy, sorrow and the feeling brain*. Vintage.

Davis, B., & Sumara, D. (2006). *Complexity and education: Inquiries into learning, teaching, and research*. Lawrence Erlbaum Associates.

de Bot, K. (2015). Rates of change: Timescales in second language development. In Z. Dornyei, P. D. MacIntyre, & A. Henry (Eds.), *Motivational dynamics in language learning* (pp. 29–37). Multilingual Matters.

de Wolf, T., & Holvoet, T. (2005). Emergence versus self-organization: Different concepts but promising when combined. In S. A. Brueckner, G. Di Marzo Serugendo, A. Karageorgos, & R. Nagpal (Eds.), *Engineering self-organising systems: Methodologies and applications* (pp. 1–15). Springer.

Denzin, N. K. (1984). *On understanding emotion*. Jossey-Bass.

Dewaele, J.-M. (2013). Personality in second language acquisition. In C. A. Chapelle (Ed.), *The encyclopedia of applied linguistics* (pp. 1–8). Wiley-Blackwell.

Dewaele, J.-M. (2019). When elephants fly: The lift-off of emotion research in applied linguistics. *The Modern Language Journal, 103*(2), 533–536.

Dewaele, J.-M. (2021). The emotional rollercoaster ride of foreign language learners and teachers: Sources and interactions of classroom emotions. In M. Simons & T. F. H. Smits (Eds.), *Language education and emotions: Research into emotions and language learners, language teachers and educational processes* (pp. 207–222). Routledge.

Dewaele, J.-M., & Alfawzan, M. (2018). Does the effect of enjoyment outweigh that of anxiety in foreign language performance? *Studies in Second Language Learning and Teaching, 8*(1), 21–45. https://doi.org/10.14746/ssllt.2018.8.1.2

Dewaele, J.-M., & Li, C. (2020). Emotions in second language acquisition: A critical review and research agenda. *Foreign Language World, 196*(1), 34–49.

Dewaele, J.-M., & MacIntyre, P. D. (2014). The two faces of Janus? Anxiety and enjoyment in the foreign language classroom. *Studies in Second Language Learning and Teaching, 4*, 237–274.

Dewaele, J.-M., & MacIntyre, P. D. (2016). Foreign language enjoyment and foreign language classroom anxiety: The right and left feet of the language learner. In P. D. MacIntyre, T. Gregersen, & S. Mercer (Eds.), *Positive psychology in SLA* (pp. 215–236). Multilingual Matters.

Dewaele, J.-M., & Thirtle, H. (2009). Why do some young learners drop foreign language? A focus on learner-internal variables. *International Journal of Bilingual Education and Bilingualism, 12*(6), 635–649.

Dewey, J. (1944). *Democracy and education*. Free Press.

Doll, W. E. (2012). Complexity and the culture of curriculum. *Complicity: An International Journal of Complexity and Education, 9*(1), 10–29.

Dörnyei, Z. (2009). The L2 motivational self system. In Z. Dörnyei & E. Ushioda (Eds.), *Motivation, language identity and the L2 self* (pp. 9–42). Multilingual Matters.

Dörnyei, Z. (2017). Conceptualizing learner characteristics in a complex, dynamic world. In L. Ortega & Z. H. Han (Eds.), *Complexity theory and language development: In celebration of Diane Larsen-Freeman* (pp. 79–96). John Benjamins Publishing Company.

Dörnyei, Z., & Ryan, S. (2015). *The psychology of the language learner revisited*. Routledge.

Dörnyei, Z., & Ushioda, E. (2009). *Motivation, language identity and the L2 self*. Multilingual Matters.

Dörnyei, Z., & Ushioda, E. (2011). *Teaching and researching motivation* (2nd ed.). Pearson Education Limited.

Dörnyei, Z., MacIntyre, P. D., & Henry, A. (2015). *Motivational dynamics in language learning*. Multilingual Matters.

Dufva, H., & Aro, M. (2015). Dialogical view on language learners' agency: Connecting intrapersonal with interpersonal. In P. Deters, X. Gao, E. R. Miller, & G. Vitanova (Eds.), *Theorizing and analyzing agency in second language learning: Interdisciplinary approaches* (pp. 37–53). Multilingual Matters.

Edwards, D. (1997). *Discourse and cognition*. SAGE Publications.

Ehrlichman, H., & Micic, D. (2012). Why do people move their eyes when they think? *Current Directions in Psychological Science, 21*(2), 96–100. https://doi.org/10.1177/0963721412436810

Ekman, P., Friesen, W. V., & Ellsworth, P. (1972). *Emotion in the human face*. Pergamon.

Elahi Shirvan, M., & Taherian, T. (2021). Relational influences of a teacher's self-disclosure on the emergence of foreign language enjoyment patterns. In M. Simons & T. F. H. Smits (Eds.), *Language education and emotions: Research into emotions and language learners, language teachers and educational processes* (pp. 136–148). Routledge.

Ellis, N. C., & Larsen-Freeman, D. (2009). *Language as a complex adaptive system*. Wiley-Blackwell.

Ellis, R. (2021). A short history of SLA: Where have we come from and where are we going? *Language Teaching, 54*(2), 190–205.

Falout, J. (2016). Past selves: Emerging motivational guides across temporal contexts. In J. King (Ed.), *The dynamic interplay between context and the language learner* (pp. 47–65). Palgrave Macmillan.

Feldman Barrett, L. (2015). Ten common misconceptions about psychological construction theories of emotion. In L. Feldman Barrett & J. A. Russell (Eds.), *The psychological construction of emotion* (pp. 45–79). Guilford Press.

References

Feldman Barrett, L. (2018). *How emotions are made: The secret life of the brain.* Pan Books.

Feldman Barrett, L., & Russell, J. A. (2015). An introduction to psychological construction. In L. Feldman Barrett & J. A. Russell (Eds.), *The psychological construction of emotion* (pp. 1–17). Guilford Press.

Finch, A. (2010). Critical incidents and language learning: Sensitivity to initial conditions. *System, 38*(3), 422–431.

Flack, W. J., & Laird, J. D. (1998). *Emotions in psychopathology: Theory and research.* Oxford University Press.

Fredrickson, B. L. (1998). What good are positive emotions? *Review of General Psychology, 2,* 300–319.

Freiermuth, M. R., & Zarrinabadi, N. (Eds.). (2020). *Technology and the psychology of second language learners and users.* Palgrave Macmillan.

Garrett, P., & Young, R. F. (2009). Theorizing affect in foreign language learning: An analysis of one learner's responses to a communicative Portuguese course. *The Modern Language Journal, 93*(2), 209–226.

Gass, S., & Mackey, A. (2000). *Stimulated recall methodology in second language research.* Lawrence Erlbaum.

Gill, S., & Thomson, G. (2017). *Human-centred education.* Routledge.

Gilmore, A. (2016). Language learning in context: Complex dynamic systems and the role of mixed methods research. In J. King (Ed.), *The dynamic interplay between context and the language learner* (pp. 194–224). Palgrave Macmillan.

Gkonou, C. (2017). Towards an ecological understanding of language anxiety. In C. Gkonou, M. Daubney, & J.-M. Dewaele (Eds.), *New insights into language anxiety: Theory, research and educational implications* (pp. 135–155). Multilingual Matters.

Gkonou, C., Daubney, M., & Dewaele, J.-M. (Eds.). (2017). *New insights into language anxiety: Theory, research and educational implications.* Multilingual Matters.

Gladwell, M. (2000). *The tipping point: How little things can make a big difference.* Little, Brown and Company.

Gleick, J. (1987). *Chaos: Making a new science.* Penguin Books.

Goetz, J. L., Keltner, D., & Simon-Thomas, E. (2010). Compassion : An evolutionary analysis and empirical review. *Psychological Bulletin, 136*(3), 351–374. https://doi.org/10.1037/a0018807

Gonzalez-Lloret, M. (2016). The construction of emotion in multilingual computer-mediated interaction. In M. T. Prior & G. Kasper (Eds.), *Emotion in multilingual interaction* (pp. 289–311). John Benjamins Publishing Company.

Goodwin, C. (2000). Action and embodiment within situated human interaction. *Journal of Pragmatics, 32*(10), 1489–1522. https://doi.org/10.1016/S0378-2166(99)00096-X

Goodwin, C. (2010). Multimodality in human interaction. *Calidoscópio, 8*(2), 85–98. https://doi.org/10.4013/cld.2010.82.01

Goodwin, C. (2018). *Co-operative action.* Cambridge University Press.

Gregersen, T., & Horwitz, E. K. (2002). Language learning and perfectionism: Anxious and non-anxious language learners' reactions to their own oral performance. *The Modern Language Journal, 86*(4), 562–570.

References

Gregersen, T., MacIntyre, P. D., & Meza, M. D. (2014). The motion of emotion: Idiodynamic case studies of learners' foreign language anxiety. *The Modern Language Journal, 98*(2), 574–588.

Gregersen, T., MacIntyre, P. D., & Olson, T. (2017). Do you see what I feel? An idiodynamic assessment of expert and peer's reading of nonverbal language anxiety cues. In C. Gkonou, M. Daubney, & J.-M. Dewaele (Eds.), *New insights into language anxiety: Theory, research and educational implications* (pp. 110–134). Multilingual Matters.

Haggis, T. (2008). "Knowledge must be contextual": Some possible implications of complexity and dynamic systems theories for educational research. *Educational Philosophy and Theory, 40*(1), 158–176.

Hall, G. (2008). An ethnographic diary study. *ELT Journal, 62*(2), 113–122.

Halquist, D., & Musanti, S. (2010). Critical incidents and reflection: Turning points that challenge the researcher and create opportunities for knowing. *International Journal of Qualitative Studies in Education, 23*(4), 449–461.

Han, Z. H., Bao, G., & Wiita, P. (2017). Energy conservation in SLA: The simplicity of a complex adaptive system. In L. Ortega & Z. H. Han (Eds.), *Complexity theory and language development: In celebration of Diane Larsen-Freeman* (pp. 209–231). John Benjamins Publishing Company.

Hiver, P., & Al-Hoorie, A. H. (2020). *Research methods for complexity in applied linguistics*. Multilingual Matters.

Horwitz, E. K. (2017). On the misreading of Horwitz, Horwitz and Cope (1986) and the need to balance anxiety research and the experiences of anxious language learners. In C. Gkonou, M. Daubney, & J.-M. Dewaele (Eds.), *New insights into language anxiety: Theory, research and educational implications* (pp. 31–47). Multilingual Matters.

Horwitz, E. K., Horwitz, M. B., & Cope, J. (1986). Foreign language classroom anxiety. *The Modern Language Journal, 70*, 125–132.

Imai, Y. (2010). Emotions in SLA: New insights from collaborative learning for an EFL classroom. *The Modern Language Journal, 94*, 278–292.

Immordino-Yang, M. H. (2016). Introduction: Why emotions are integral to learning. In M. H. Immordino-Yang (Ed.), *Emotions, learning, and the brain: Exploring the educational implications of affective neuroscience* (pp. 17–24). Norton.

Immordino-Yang, M. H., & Damasio, A. R. (2016). We feel, therefore we learn: The relevance of affective and social neuroscience to education. In M. H. Immordino-Yang (Ed.), *Emotions, learning, and the brain: Exploring the educational implications of affective neuroscience* (pp. 27–42). Norton.

Immordino-Yang, M. H., & Fischer, K. W. (2016). Neuroscience bases of learning. In M. H. Immordino-Yang (Ed.), *Emotions, learning, and the brain: Exploring the educational implications of affective neuroscience* (pp. 79–92). Norton.

Irie, K., & Ryan, S. (2015). Study abroad and the dynamics of change in learner L2 self-concept. In Z. Dornyei, P. D. MacIntyre, & A. Henry (Eds.), *Motivational dynamics in language learning* (pp. 343–366). Multilingual Matters.

Izard, C. E. (2010). The many meanings/aspects of emotion: Definitions, functions, activation, and regulation. *Emotion Review, 2*(4), 363–370. https://doi.org/10.1177/1754073910374661

References

Järvenoja, H., & Järvelä, S. (2013). Regulating emotions together for motivated collaboration. In M Baker, J. Andriessen, & S. Järevelä (Eds.), *Affective learning together: Social and emotional dimensions of collaborative learning2* (pp. 162–181). Routledge.

Jefferson, G. (2004). Glossary of transcript symbols with an introduction. In G. H. Lerner (Ed.), *Conversation analysis: Studies from the first generation* (pp. 13–23). John Benjamins.

Juarrero, A. (2002). *Dynamics in action: Intentional behavior as a complex system* (1st MIT Pr). MIT Press.

Kauffman, S. (2008). *Reinventing the sacred*. Basic Books.

Keltner, D., & Shiota, M. (2003). New displays and new emotions: A commentary on Rozin and Cohen. *Emotion, 3*(1), 86–91.

Keltner, D., Sauter, D., Tracy, J., & Cowen, A. (2019). Emotional expression: Advances in basic emotion theory. *Journal of Nonverbal Behavior, 43*(2), 133–160. https://doi.org/10.1007/s10919-019-00293-3.Emotional

King, J. (Ed.). (2016). *The dynamic interplay between context and the language learner*. Palgrave Macmillan.

King, J., & Smith, L. (2017). Social anxiety and silence in Japan's tertiary foreign language classrooms. In C. Gkonou, M. Daubney, & J.-M. Dewaele (Eds.), *New insights into language anxiety: Theory, research and educational implications* (pp. 91–109). Multilingual Matters.

Kramsch, C. (2002a). Introduction: "How can we tell the dancer from the dance?" In C. Kramsch (Ed.), *Language acquisition and language socialization: Ecological perspectives* (pp. 1–30). Continuum.

Kramsch, C. (Ed.). (2002b). *Language acquisition and language socialization: Ecological perspectives*. Continuum.

Larsen-Freeman, D. (1997). Chaos/complexity science and second language acquisition. *Applied Linguistics, 18*(2), 141–165.

Larsen-Freeman, D. (2017). Complexity theory: The lessons continue. In L. Ortega & Z. H. Han (Eds.), *Complexity theory and language development: In celebration of Diane Larsen-Freeman* (pp. 11–50). John Benjamins Publishing Company.

Larsen-Freeman, D. (2019). Thoughts on the launching of a new journal: A complex dynamic systems perspective. *Journal for the Psychology of Language Learning, 1*, 67–82.

Larsen-Freeman, D., & Cameron, L. (2008). *Complex systems and applied linguistics*. Oxford University Press.

Lemke, J. L. (2000). Across the scales of time: Artifacts, activities, and meanings in ecosocial systems. *Mind, Culture, and Activity, 7*(4), 273–290. https://doi.org/10.1207/S15327884MCA0704_03

Lemke, J. L. (2013). Feeling and meaning in the social ecology of learning: Lessons from play and games. In M Baker, J. Andriessen, & S. Jarvela (Eds.), *Affective learning together: Social and emotional dimensions of collaborative learning* (pp. 71–94). Routledge.

Machi, S. (2012). How repetition works in Japanese and English conversation: Introducing different cultural orientations towards conversation. *The English Linguistic Society of Japan JELS, 29*, 260–266.

References

Machi, S. (2019). Managing relationships through repetition: How repetition creates ever-shifting relationships in Japanese conversation. *Pragmatics*, *29*(1), 57–81. https://doi.org/10.1075/prag.17021.mac

Machi, S. (2020). "Braid structure" conversations: Development of informal triadic conversation in Japanese. *The Japanese Journal of Language in Society*, *22*(2), 15–29.

MacIntyre, P. D. (2012). The idiodynamic method: A closer look at the dynamics of communication traits. *Communication Research Reports*, *29*(4), 361–367. https://doi.org/10.1080/08824096.2012.723274

MacIntyre, P. D. (2017). An overview of language anxiety research and trends in its development. In C. Gkonou, M. Daubney, & J.-M. Dewaele (Eds.), *New insights into language anxiety: Theory, research and educational implications* (pp. 11–30). Multilingual Matters.

MacIntyre, P. D., & Gardner, R. C. (1994). The subtle effects of language anxiety on cognitive processing in the second language. *Language Learning*, *44*(2), 283–305.

MacIntyre, P. D., & Gregersen, T. (2012). Affect: The role of language anxiety and other emotions in language learning. In S. Mercer, S. Ryan, & M. Williams (Eds.), *Psychology for language learning: Insights from research, theory and practice* (pp. 103–118). Palgrave Macmillan.

MacIntyre, P. D., & Legatto, J. J. (2011). A dynamic system approach to willingness to communicate: Developing an idiodynamic method to capture rapidly changing affect. *Applied Linguistics*, *32*(2), 149–171. https://doi.org/10.1093/applin/amq037

MacIntyre, P. D., & Vincze, L. (2017). Positive and negative emotions underlie motivation for L2 learning. *Studies in Second Language Learning and Teaching*, *7*(1), 61–88. https://doi.org/10.14746/ssllt.2017.7.1.4

MacIntyre, P. D., Dörnyei, Z., & Henry, A. (2015). Conclusion: Hot enough to be cool: The promise of dynamic systems research. In Z. Dörnyei, P. D. MacIntyre, & A. Henry (Eds.), *Motivational dynamics in language learning* (pp. 419–429). Multilingual Matters.

MacIntyre, P. D., Gregersen, T., & Mercer, S. (2016). *Positive psychology in SLA* (P. D. MacIntyre, T. Gregersen, & S. Mercer, Eds.). Multilingual Matters.

MacIntyre, P. D., Mercer, S., & Gregersen, T. (2021). Reflections on researching dynamics in language learning psychology. In R. J. Sampson & R. S. Pinner (Eds.), *Complexity perspectives on researching language learner and teacher psychology* (pp. 15–34). Multilingual Matters.

Matsumoto, D., Yoo, S. H., Hirayama, S., & Petrova, G. (2005). Development and validation of a measure of display rule knowledge: The display rule assessment inventory. *Emotion*, *5*, 23–40.

Matsumoto, D., Yoo, S. H., & Fontaine, J. (2008). Mapping expressive differences around the world: The relationship between emotional display rules and individualism versus collectivism. *Journal of Cross-Cultural Psychology*, *39*(1), 55–74.

McAdams, D. P. (2010). The problem of meaning in personality psychology from the standpoints of dispositional traits, characteristic adaptations, and life stories. *The Japanese Journal of Personality*, *18*(3), 173–186. https://doi.org/10.2132/personality.18.173

References

McAdams, D. P., & Pals, J. L. (2006). A new big five: Fundamental principles for an integrative science of personality. *American Psychologist, 61*(3), 204–217.
McNiff, J., & Whitehead, J. (2011). *All you need to know about action research* (2nd ed.). SAGE.
Méndez López, M. G., & Peña Aguilar, A. (2013). Emotions as learning enhancers of foreign language learning motivation. *Profile: Issues in Teachers' Professional Development, 15*(1), 109–124. http://dialnet.unirioja.es/servlet/articulo?codigo=4858457&info=resumen&idioma=SPA
Mercer, S. (2013). Towards a complexity-informed pedagogy for language learning. *Revista Brasileira de Linguística Aplicada, 13*(2), 375–398.
Mesquita, B. (2010). Emoting: A contextualized process. In B. Mesquita, L. Feldman Barrett, & E. R. Smith (Eds.), *The mind in context* (pp. 83–104). Guilford Press.
Mesquita, B., & Boiger, M. (2014). Emotions in context: A socio-dynamic model of emotions. *Emotion Review, 6*(4), 298–302.
Miyahara, M. (2015). *Emerging self-identities and emotion in foreign language learning: A narrative-oriented approach*. Multilingual Matters.
Morin, E. (2008). *On complexity*. Hampton Press.
Murphey, T. (2021). *Voicing learning*. Candlin & Mynard.
Murphey, T., & Iswanti, S. N. (2014). Surprising humanity! Comparing ideal classmates in two countries. *ETAS Journal, 31*(2), 33–35.
Murphey, T., Falout, J., Fukuda, T., & Fukada, Y. (2014). Socio-dynamic motivating through idealizing classmates. *System, 45*, 242–253. https://doi.org/10.1016/j.system.2014.06.004
Murray, G., Gao, X., & Lamb, T. (2011). *Identity, motivation and autonomy in language learning*. Multilingual Matters.
Nitta, R. (2013). Understanding motivational evolution in the EFL classroom: A longitudinal study from a dynamic systems perspective. In M. T. Apple, D. Da Silva, & T. Fellner (Eds.), *Language learning motivation in Japan* (pp. 268–290). Multilingual Matters.
Nitta, R., & Nakata, Y. (2021). Understanding complexity in language classrooms: A retrodictive approach to researching class climate. In R. J. Sampson & R. S. Pinner (Eds.), *Complexity perspectives on researching language learner and teacher psychology* (pp. 174–188). Multilingual Matters.
Norris, S. (2004). *Analyzing multimodal interaction: A methodological framework*. Routledge.
Norris, S. (2011). *Identity in interaction: Introducing multimodal interaction analysis*. De Gruyter Mouton.
Norris, S. (2020). *Multimodal theory and methodology: For the analysis of (inter)action and identity*. Routledge.
Norton, B. (2000). *Identity and language learning: Gender, ethnicity and educational change*. Longman.
Norton, B., & Toohey, K. (2001). Changing perspectives on good language learners. *TESOL Quarterly, 35*(2), 307–322.
Nunan, D., & Bailey, K. M. (2009). *Exploring second language classroom research: A comprehensive guide*. Heinle.

Oades-Sese, G. V, Matthews, T. A., & Lewis, M. (2014). Shame and pride and their effects on student achievement. In R. Pekrun & L. Linnenbrink-Garcia (Eds.), *International Handbook of Emotions in Education* (pp. 246–264). Routledge.

Onwuegbuzie, A. J., & Daniel, L. G. (2003). Typology of analytical and interpretational errors in quantitative and qualitative educational research. In *Current Issues in Education* (Vol. 6, Issue 2). http://cie.ed.asu.edu/volume6/number2/

Ortega, L., & Han, Z. H. (Eds.). (2017a). *Complexity theory and language development: In celebration of Diane Larsen-Freeman*. John Benjamins Publishing Company.

Ortega, L., & Han, Z. H. (2017b). Introduction. In L. Ortega & Z. H. Han (Eds.), *Complexity theory and language development: In celebration of Diane Larsen-Freeman* (pp. 1–10). John Benjamins Publishing Company.

Osberg, D., Biesta, G., & Cilliers, P. (2008). From representation to emergence: Complexity's challenge to the epistemology of schooling. *Educational Philosophy and Theory*, *40*(1), 213–227.

Oxford, R. L. (2014). What we can learn about strategies, language learning, and life from two extreme cases. *Studies in Second Language Learning and Teaching*, *4*(4), 593–615.

Oxford, R. L. (2016). Toward a psychology of well-being for language learners: The "EMPATHICS" vision. In P. D. MacIntyre, T. Gregersen, & S. Mercer (Eds.), *Positive psychology in SLA* (pp. 10–87). Multilingual Matters.

Oxford, R. L., & Gkonou, C. (2021). Working with the complexity of language learners' emotions and emotion regulation strategies. In R. J. Sampson & R. S. Pinner (Eds.), *Complexity perspectives on researching language learner and teacher psychology* (pp. 52–67). Multilingual Matters.

Oxford, R. L., Meng, Y., Zhou, Y., Sung, J., & Jain, R. (2007). Uses of adversity: Moving beyond L2 learning crises. In A. Barfield & S. Brown (Eds.), *Reconstructing autonomy in language education: Inquiry and innovation* (pp. 131–142). Palgrave Macmillan.

Pallotti, G. (2021). Cratylus' silence: On the philosophy and methodology of complex dynamic systems theory in SLA. *Second Language Research*, online fir, 1–13. https://doi.org/10.1177/0267658321992451

Pavlenko, A. (2013). The affective turn in SLA: From "affective factors" to "language desire" and "commodification of affect". In D. Gabrys-Barker & J. Bielska (Eds.), *The affective dimension in second language acquisition* (pp. 3–28). Multilingual Matters.

Pawlak, M., Kruk, M., Zawodniak, J., & Pasikowski, S. (2020a). Investigating factors responsible for boredom in English classes: The case of advanced learners. *System*, *91*. https://doi.org/10.1016/j.system.2020.102259

Pawlak, M., Zawodniak, J., & Kruk, M. (2020b). *Boredom in the foreign language classroom: A micro-perspective*. Springer.

Pawlak, M., Zawodniak, J., & Kruk, M. (2021). Individual trajectories of boredom in learning English as a foreign language at the university level: Insights from three students' self-reported experience. *Innovation in Language Learning and Teaching*, *15*(3), 263–278.

Pekrun, R. (2014). *Emotions and learning*. International Academy of Education.
Pekrun, R., & Linnenbrink-Garcia, L. (2014). Introduction to emotions in education. In R. Pekrun & L. Linnenbrink-Garcia (Eds.), *International handbook of emotions in education* (pp. 1–10). Routledge.
Peragine, M. (2019). Idealizing L2 classmates to combat amotivation, calculate motivational deviations, and foster group cohesiveness. *New Directions in Teaching and Learning English* Discussion, 7, 168–178.
Phelps, R. (2005). The potential of reflective journals in studying complexity "in action." *Complicity: An International Journal of Complexity and Education*, 2(1), 37–54.
Philp, J., Adams, R., & Iwashita, N. (2014). *Peer interaction and second language learning*. Routledge.
Pinner, R. S. (2016a). *Reconceptualising authenticity for English as a global language*. Multilingual Matters.
Pinner, R. S. (2016b). Trouble in paradise: Self-assessment and the Tao. *Language Teaching Research*, 20(2), 181–195.
Pinner, R. S. (2019). *Authenticity and teacher-student motivational synergy: A narrative of language teaching*. Routledge.
Pinner, R. S., & Sampson, R. J. (2021). Humanizing TESOL research through the lens of complexity thinking. *TESOL Quarterly*, 55(2), 633–642. https://doi.org/10.1002/tesq.604
Plutchik, R. (2001). The nature of emotions: Human emotions have deep evolutionary roots, a fact that may explain their complexity and provide tools for clinical practice. *American Scientist*, 89(4), 344–350.
Porto, M. (2007). Learning diaries in the English as a Foreign Language classroom: A tool for accessing learners' perceptions of lessons and developing learner autonomy and reflection. *Foreign Language Annals*, 40(4), 672–696.
Prior, M. T. (2016a). Contextualizing emotion in multilingual interaction: Theoretical and methodological perspectives. In M. T. Prior & G. Kasper (Eds.), *Emotion in multilingual interaction* (pp. 1–28). John Benjamins Publishing Company.
Prior, M. T. (2016b). *Emotion and discourse in L2 narrative research*. Multilingual Matters.
Prior, M. T. (2019). Elephants in the room: An "affective turn," or just feeling our way? *The Modern Language Journal*, 103(2), 516–527.
Prior, M. T., & Kasper, G. (Eds.). (2016). *Emotion in multilingual interaction*. John Benjamins Publishing Company.
Reeve, J. (1993). The face of interest. *Motivation and Emotion*, 17(4), 353–375. https://doi.org/10.1007/BF00992325
Reisenzein, R., Junge, M., Studtmann, M., & Huber, O. (2014). Observational approaches to the measurement of emotions. In R. Pekrun & L. Linnenbrink-Garcia (Eds.), *International handbook of emotions in education* (pp. 580–606). Routledge.
Rendell, J., & Denison, R. (2018). Introducing Studio Ghibli. *East Asian Journal of Popular Culture*, 4(1), 5–14.
Richards, K. (2006). "Being the teacher": Identity and classroom conversation. *Applied Linguistics*, 27(1), 51–77.

Rodgers, C. (2002). Defining reflection: Another look at Dewey and reflective thinking. *Teachers College Record*, *104*(4), 842–866.

Rose, H. (2020). Diaries and journals: Collecting insider perspectives in second language research. In J. McKinley & H. Rose (Eds.), *Routledge handbook of research methods in applied linguistics* (pp. 348–356). Routledge.

Rozin, P., & Cohen, A. B. (2003). High frequency of facial expressions corresponding to confusion, concentration, and worry in an analysis of naturally occurring facial expressions of Americans. *Emotion*, *3*(1), 68–75.

Russell, J. A. (2015). My psychological constructionist perspective, with a focus on conscious affective experience. In L. Feldman Barrett & J. A. Russell (Eds.), *The psychological construction of emotion* (pp. 183–208). Guilford Press.

Ruusuvuori, J. (2012). Emotion, affect and conversation. In J. Sidnell & T. Stivers (Eds.), *The handbook of conversation analysis* (pp. 330–349). Wiley-Blackwell.

Ryan, R. M., & Deci, E. L. (2002). Overview of self-determination theory: An organismic dialectical perspective. In E. L. Deci & R. M. Ryan (Eds.), *Handbook of Self-Determination Research* (pp. 3–33). University of Rochester Press.

Ryan, R. M., & Deci, E. L. (2017). *Self-determination theory: Basic psychological needs in motivation, development, and wellness*. Guilford Press.

Saldana, J. (2016). *The coding manual for qualitative researchers* (3rd ed.). Sage Publications.

Sampson, R. J. (2016a). *Complexity in classroom foreign language learning motivation: A practitioner perspective from Japan*. Multilingual Matters.

Sampson, R. J. (2016b). EFL teacher motivation in-situ: Co-adaptive processes, openness and relational motivation over interacting timescales. *Studies in Second Language Learning and Teaching*, *6*(2), 293–318. https://doi.org/10.14746/ssllt.2016.6.2.6

Sampson, R. J. (2017). Expectations and dreams: Industry and student ideas about future English use. *OnCUE Journal*, *10*(1), 21–38. https://doi.org/10.1002/ana.23528/pdf

Sampson, R. J. (2018). Complexity in acting on images of ideal classmates in the L2 classroom. *Konin Language Studies*, *6*(4), 387–410. https://doi.org/10.30438/ksj.2018.6.4.2

Sampson, R. J. (2019a). Openness to messages about English as a foreign language: Working with learners to uncover purpose to study. *Language Teaching Research*, *23*(1), 126–142. https://doi.org/10.1177/1362168817712074

Sampson, R. J. (2019b). Real people with real experiences: The emergence of classroom L2 study feelings over interacting timescales. *System*, *84*, 14–23. https://doi.org/10.1016/j.system.2019.05.001

Sampson, R. J. (2020). The feeling classroom: Diversity of feelings in instructed L2 learning. *Innovation in Language Learning and Teaching*, *14*(3), 203–217. https://doi.org/10.1080/17501229.2018.1553178

Sampson, R. J. (2021). Interacting levels and timescales in the emergence of feelings in the L2 classroom. In R. J. Sampson & R. S. Pinner (Eds.), *Complexity perspectives on researching language learner and teacher psychology* (pp. 35–51). Multilingual Matters.

Sampson, R. J. (2022). From darkness to light: Teacher immunity and the emergence of relatedness with students. In Y. Kimura, L. Yang, T.-Y. Kim, & Y. Nakata (Eds.), *Language teacher motivation, autonomy and development in East Asia* (pp. 71–90). Springer.
Sampson, R. J., & Pinner, R. S. (Eds.). (2021). *Complexity perspectives on researching language learner and teacher psychology*. Multilingual Matters.
Sampson, R. J., & Yoshida, R. (2020). Emergence of divergent L2 feelings through the co-adapted social context of online chat. *Linguistics and Education*, 60, 1–10. https://doi.org/10.1016/j.linged.2020.100861
Sampson, R. J., & Yoshida, R. (2021). L2 feelings through interaction in a Japanese-English online chat exchange. *Innovation in Language Learning and Teaching*, 15(2), 131–142. https://doi.org/10.1080/17501229.2019.1710514
Schumann, J. H. (2015). Foreword. In Z. Dörnyei, P. D. MacIntyre, & A. Henry (Eds.), *Motivational dynamics in language learning* (pp. xv–xix). Multilingual Matters.
Shiota, M., & Kalat, J. (2018). *Emotion* (3rd ed.). Oxford University Press.
Shuman, V., & Scherer, K. R. (2014). Concepts and structures of emotions. In *International handbook of emotions in education* (pp. 13–35). Routledge.
Simpson, K., & Rose, H. (2021). Complexity as a valid approach in "messy" classroom contexts: Promoting more "ecologically rich" research on the psychology of L2 listening. In R. J. Sampson & R. S. Pinner (Eds.), *Complexity perspectives on researching language learner and teacher psychology* (pp. 136–151). Multilingual Matters.
Simsek, E., & Dörnyei, Z. (2017). Anxiety and L2 self-images: The "anxious self." In C. Gkonou, M. Daubney, & J.-M. Dewaele (Eds.), *New insights into language anxiety: Theory, research and educational implications* (pp. 51–69). Multilingual Matters.
Smith, L., & King, J. (2021). Researching the complexity of silence in second-language classrooms. In R. J. Sampson & R. S. Pinner (Eds.), *Complexity perspectives on researching language learner and teacher psychology* (pp. 86–102). Multilingual Matters.
Sorenson, G. (1989). The relationship among teachers' self-disclosure statements, students' perceptions, and affective learning. *Communication Education*, 38, 259–276.
Taylor, F. (2013). *Self and identity in adolescent foreign language learning*. Multilingual Matters.
Tripp, D. (1993). *Critical incidents in teaching: Developing professional judgment*. Routledge.
Turner, J. H., & Stets, J. E. (2005). *The sociology of emotions*. Cambridge University Press.
Urdan, T. (2014). Understanding teacher motivation: What is known and what more there is to learn. In P. W. Richardson, S. A. Karabenick, & H. M. G. Watt (Eds.), *Teacher Motivation: Theory and Practice* (pp. 227–246). Routledge.
Ushioda, E. (2009). A person-in-context relational view of emergent motivation, self and identity. In Z. Dörnyei & E. Ushioda (Eds.), *Motivation, language identity and the L2 self* (pp. 215–228). Multilingual Matters.

Ushioda, E. (2011a). Context matters: A brief commentary on the papers by Housen et al. and Munoz. *International Review of Applied Linguistics in Language Teaching, 49*(2), 187–189.

Ushioda, E. (2011b). Motivating learners to speak as themselves. In G. Murray, X. Gao, & T. Lamb (Eds.), *Identity, motivation and autonomy in language learning* (pp. 11–24). Multilingual Matters.

Ushioda, E. (2015). Context and complex dynamic systems theory. In Z. Dörnyei, P. D. MacIntyre, & A. Henry (Eds.), *Motivational dynamics in language learning* (pp. 47–54). Multilingual Matters.

Ushioda, E. (2016). Language learning motivation through a small lens: A research agenda. *Language Teaching, 49*(4), 564–577.

Ushioda, E. (2020). *Language learning motivation: An ethical agenda for research*. Oxford University Press.

Ushioda, E. (2021). Doing complexity research in the language classroom: A commentary. In R. J. Sampson & R. S. Pinner (Eds.), *Complexity perspectives on researching language learner and teacher psychology* (pp. 269–283). Multilingual Matters.

van Lier, L. (2004). *The ecology and semiotics of language learning: A sociocultural perspective*. Kluwer Academic Publishers.

Vijayakumar, N., & Pfeifer, J. H. (2020). Self-disclosure during adolescence: Exploring the means, targets, and types of personal exchanges. *Current Opinion in Psychology, 31*, 135–140. https://doi.org/10.1016/j.copsyc.2019.08.005

Wiggins, S. (2017). *Discursive psychology: Theory, method and applications*. SAGE Publications.

Witherington, D. C. (2011). Taking emergence seriously: The centrality of circular causality for dynamic systems approaches to development. *Human Development, 54*(2), 66–92. https://doi.org/10.1159/000326814

Yashima, T. (2002). Willingness to communicate in a second language: The Japanese EFL context. *The Modern Language Journal, 86*(i), 54–66.

Yashima, T. (2021). Nested systems and their interactions: Dynamic WTC in the classroom. In R. J. Sampson & R. S. Pinner (Eds.), *Complexity perspectives on researching language learner and teacher psychology* (pp. 68–85). Multilingual Matters.

Yashima, T., & Arao, K. (2015). Understanding EFL learners' motivational dynamics: A three-level model from a dynamic systems and sociocultural perspective. In Z. Dornyei, P. D. MacIntyre, & A. Henry (Eds.), *Motivational dynamics in language learning* (pp. 285–314). Multilingual Matters.

Yoshida, R. (2020). Emotional scaffolding in text chats between Japanese language learners and native Japanese speakers. *Foreign Language Annals, 53*(3), 505–526.

Zimmerman, D. H. (1998). Discoursal identities and social identities. In C. Antaki & S. Widdicombe (Eds.), *Identities in talk* (pp. 87–106). Sage.

Index

agency 4, 28, 43, 72, 77–78, 83–84, 93
anxiety: definition of (general) **32**; definition of (language) 49; displays of 68–69; general 2, 49–50, 55, 65, 66, 82–83, 101; language 6, 12n1, 13–21, 34, 49–52, 66, 81–83, 98

Boiger, M. 4, 47, 55, 63, 79, 91
boredom 6, 14, 16–17, 31, 33, 89

Cilliers, P. 54, 61, 63, 92
circular causality 26, 82
class climate 2, 26, 39, 41, 47, 96; *see also* multiple threading
co-adaptation 54, 57, 60, 62, 93, 100
complexity perspective 6–10, 31, 57, 63, 72, 77, 86–89, 95; *see also* circular causality; co-adaptation; dynamics, in complexity; emergence; lock-in; non-linearity; openness; self-organization; timescales
constructed emotion, theory of 3, 79, 91
critical incidents 46–47, 63
cultural practices 4, 57, 60–61, 100

Denzin, N. 9, 22, 44, 56, 60, 71, 101–103
Dewaele, J-M. 1, 13–15, 50, 52, 70, 83, 87–88, 91
disappointment 17, 73, 77–78; across class group 33–35; definition of **32**; and lesson segments 37–38; in self 64–66; as a topic 55–57, 60
diversity of emotions 17, 30, 38–41, 95–96, 100

Dörnyei, Z. 7, 20, 27, 35, 70, 83–84, 92, 102
dynamics 21–22, 35, 43, 69–70, 79–80, 89, 95–96; in complexity 6–10, 54, 82, 86, 92; in research methods 16–18, 28–30, 63, 90, 94n1

embarrassment 2–5, 51, 58, 61, 68–69, 75
emergence 26, 52, 82; definition of 54
emotional intersubjectivity 22, 56, 60, 101–103
emotions: definition 2–4; education and 1–4, 44, 98–99; feelings (definition) 3; focus 2–3, 16–17, 20, 22, 91; functions 4, 45; valence 3, 38, 55
encouragement 51–52, 67, 70, 79
enjoyment 50, 70, 73, 76; across class group 34–35; definition of **32**; expanding L2 research of 15–16, 98, 101; and L2 study 50, 52; and lesson segments 37–38
excitement 34, 74, 76, 81–82, 84; definition of **32**
expressions: bodily **51**, 66–69, 77–80; definition of 3, 45; facial **51**, 60–61, 66–69, 75–80; *see also* posture; vocal bursts

Gkonou, C. 3, 20–21, 38, 103
Gregersen, T. 15, 18, 51, 66, 68–69, 81
groups 62, 64–69, 73–74, 78–84, 102; and emotional regulation 4, 22–23, 45; *see also* class climate

Index

historical perspective 44, 46, 49, 61, 63, 73–74, 79–81
holistic view 2, 8, 20–21, 84
Horwitz, E. 6, 14, 21, 52, 69, 81
humanistic perspectives 8, 36–38, 43, 88, 92, 96

identity 20; second language 22, 43, 56–57, 81–82, 84; transportable 52–53, 56–57, 60–61, 68, 73, 76–77, 100–101
idiodynamic method 17–18, 50, 94n1
Imai, Y. 22–23, 44, 46, 56, 60
interest 17–18, 22, 50–52, **58**, 60–61, 73, 80; across class group 34–35; definition of **32**
introspective data collection 23, 28, 46–47, 56, 100

journals 28–31, 42n1, 46–47, 88, 94n1

Keltner, D. 45, 51, 60, 68–69, 76, 78

Larsen-Freeman, D. 7–8, 44, 72, 77
Lemke, J. 31, 44, 78, 82, 93
lock-in 70, 83

MacIntyre, P. 7, 14–15, 18–19, 34, 49–50, 69–70, 83, 89; on complexity 9, 63, 91
Mesquita, B. 4, 55, 57, 63, 79, 91
Morin, E. 6–7, 77, 86, 95
motivation 31, 50, 57, 60, 65, 73–74, 81–83; across class group 35; definition of **32**; and research into correspondence with emotions 19–20
multiple threading 38–42, 93, 96

narrative research 19–20, 23, 46
neuroscience 1, 3, 41, 96
Nitta, R. 26, 39, 41
non-linearity 52–53, 84
noticing 18, 54, 64–67, 81–82, 99

observatory data collection 18, 45–48, 60, 87–90, 92
online L2 study emotions 14, 17, 23, 90, 99
openness 49, 92–93
Oxford, R. 3, 34, 98, 103

Pavlenko, A. 6–7, 13, 41, 87–88
Pawlak, M. 16, 31, 89
personality 20–21, 55–56, 65, 72, 81–85, 93, 102
person-in-context relational view 43–44, 57, 60, 62, 101
Pinner, R. S. 64, 97–98, 101
positive psychology 13, 15, 17, 34, 70, 98
posture 3, 51–52, 57–59, 66–69, 75–80, 90
practitioner research 8, 25, 46, 48, 87, 89, 94n1, 95, 98
Prior, M. 44–45, 48, 87, 90
progress: across class group 34–35; definition of **32**; sense of 73–74, 81, 84

relatedness 6, 50, 52, 73, 76–77; definition of **32**, 50
relationships (interpersonal) 4, 33, 53–56, 63, 70, 79–80, 95

Sampson, R. J. 25, 29, 39, 82, 95, 99; on classroom emotions 6, 9, 16–20, 31, 56; on complexity 8, 54, 92, 102; on motivation 16, 27, 57, 74; on online emotions 6, 17, 23, 90; on practitioner research 46
self-disclosure 70, 100–101
self-organization 26, 39, 54, 88, 103
sensemaking 20, 46, 65, 79, 82, 84
shame 64–65, 82–83
significant episodes 46–48, 63–64, 88–89, 96
silence 41, 64, 66, 68–69, 83, 105
simplicity 6–7, 43
small lens approach 45–48, 63, 70, 88, 90, 93, 102
social context 2–4, 9–10, 21–23, 43–46, 54, 87–93, 101–103; discursive analysis of 50–52, 57–62, 66–70, 74–80
support (in interaction) 16, 45, 52, 60–62, 68–70
sympathy **32**, **34**, **58**, 61–62, **75**, 77, 101

textbook exercises 27–28, 36–38, 64–65, 79–80, 96–98

timescales 16, 20, 35, 49, 78, 82, 91–93
transcribing 45, 47–48, 90–91, 105

Ushioda, E.: on complexity 8, 57, 63, 88; on identity 9, 43–44, 52, 100–101; on motivation 35, 43–44, 100–101; on practitioner research 25, 89; on social context 11, 44–48, 54, 60

vocal bursts 45, 48, 51, 57, 60–61, 93

Yashima, T. 35, 41, 80

For Product Safety Concerns and Information please contact our EU representative GPSR@taylorandfrancis.com
Taylor & Francis Verlag GmbH, Kaufingerstraße 24, 80331 München, Germany

www.ingramcontent.com/pod-product-compliance
Lightning Source LLC
Chambersburg PA
CBHW051753230426
43670CB00012B/2266